CAN YOU FEEL IT?

T0272130

SET MARGINS' #1

INDEX

INDEX

Dear,

We touch the world, we sense its objects, but these sensations disappear all too quickly, leaving us with fleeting impressions. Our sense of touch is characteristic and yet we know very little about it.

Today, tactility asks for attention. In the high-tech and knowledge-driven society we live in, the tactile is being increasingly recognised as a quality and processed accordingly. Now, even more than in the pre-digital era, tactility is something we can become conscious of, if only because the variety of tactile materials has continued to increase. By being more aware of our tactility, we can learn to better define it and discover its richness.

Tactility is a physical sensation and at the same time it is a mental experience; it is ambiguous in nature. In addition, the tactile object can both be hand-crafted from basic materials or produced using sophisticated technological and/or biochemical processes. In its growing complexity, tactility becomes ever more hybrid: layered in material, making the flowing sense of the tactile world increasingly ambiguous. What do we actually feel when we touch things? What feels like a natural material, no longer needs to be natural at all. We become increasingly alienated from the uncomplicated tactility that existed before the advance of hybrid objects, unless we consciously reach for its changing appearance. Is it old-fashioned to hold on to familiar things? Should we just grasp things, should we actually feel them, or should we contemplate them and look for words to describe them? Is tactility a trick of the mind or is it a sensual quality that we can seize upon? What does beauty feel like and when does beauty feel 'right'? Can we express this in language or trace it out on paper?

During a residency at the graphic workshop of the Frans Masereel Centrum, six artists were challenged to produce a graphic sample or the essence of the tactility featuring in their oeuvre. This has resulted in a variety of works that reveal the diversity and range of tactility through the artists' distinctive handwriting or language. Tactility also touches thinkers and writers. In the light of their contemplations, tactility proves to be perceptible on the surface of the skin while remaining intangible underneath. The exact qualities of touch are harder to read than the context in which it is acting. The desire to make contact is strong and appeals to our sensitivity; in a changing material environment this is cause for considerable strain. That is exactly why cultural production in our present time is so exciting. These extraordinary gestures towards the tactile world are being presented in an emotive and anecdotical manner. They provide access to a spectrum where you can join them in tracing tactility's ambiguous position.
Can you feel it?

Freek Lomme, initiator and host of the project.

THE ARTISTIC PROCESS AT THE FRANS MASEREEL CENTRE

SEMÂ BERIKOVIC

"I think natural processes are constantly
at play in our cultural constructs.
With this thought in the back of my head
I often try to make works that embrace their
own temporality."

Semâ Bekirovic in an
interview with Rachel Stern

Semâ Bekirovic tackles the ongoing struggle between culture and nature
with wit and offbeat intelligence.* Like reality, her work is a universe of
temporary constellations wherein objects, people, animals and/or chemical
reactions trigger one another into acting out their parts, combining aspects
of human reason through cultivation and natural will by chance.
    *quote by Skye Sherwi.

FL: How did you initially feel about the request for a "concentrate / sample" of the tactile in your work and what was your first idea to process it into a piece?

SB: To me, tactility is an almost magical phenomenon. In a way, truly physically touching something is impossible (atoms being incapable of actual physical contact). On the other hand physical contact always entails a kind of dissolving: the border between two bodies gets blurred by the transference of heat. I attempted to zoom in on this in a number of works.

FL: How did you start working at FMC?

SB: For this project, I made silk screens and collaborated with a bunch of snails. Snails are obviously extremely tactile: where we mostly touch the world around us only with the very ends of our bodies, the snail does so with a maximum of body surface. When the snails crawl across the freshly made prints, their slime trails dissolve the (water soluble) paint, leaving coloured trails on the paper.

FL: How do you feel about tactility in the contemporary and (in what way) does this inspire your work?

SB: In my video triptych *The Radiance of Sensible Heat* (2015), for instance, there's a blind masseur attempting to identify clay sculptures (of a hand, an eye and an ear) by touch. By recording this with a thermal imaging camera the focus is directed to the transfer of body heat from masseur to sculptures; we see them gradually light up as they get warmer. Another work, *Relational Voodoo* (2015), explores our physical relationship to objects and focuses on the bits of our identity we leave on everything we touch by employing forensic methods to show the fingerprints that were left on objects I bought at flea markets.

MATTHIEU BLANCHARD

"Physical and chemical reactions interest
me. In practice, it's almost alchemy.
The result is not important, process matters.
I let the material do what it wants,
it stabilizes itself without my intervention."

Matthieu Blanchard in an
interview with Samy Abraham

Before they become paintings, the tableaux of Blanchard often already
lived a long life undergoing manipulation in different stages. Here, chemical
and natural reactions inspire the result. Serendipity is combined with
experience, accumulates knowledge of its alchemy and allows exploring
the flow of aesthetics.

FL: How did you initially feel about the request for a "concentrate / sample" of the tactile in your work and what was your first idea to process it into a piece?

MB: The principle of concentrate or sample reminds me of a Petri dish. A solution is put in a glass plate and with different reactions we observe a change of state or form. Sometimes the observed subject tries to escape from the box and acts by itself, it gets out of control. All the works I made at Frans Masereel Centrum resulted from these experiences.

I believe that dead matter does not exist. Everything moves, even when it is invisible to the naked eye. When I make a painting, I submit the matter to a test battery, sometimes I even torture the matter (by cutting or sanding it...). Sometimes these processes lead to an abstract form which does not let glimpse what it really is. The matter wants to keep its secret. My desire is to understand what happened, what the matter really hides, and to reveal its living character in the end.

FL: How did you start working at FMC?

MB: I arrived at Frans Masereel Centrum with texts, works in progress and a portable studio (paints, brushes, chemicals,...). The starting point of my research was a text by Gilles Deleuze titled *Francis Bacon, The Logic of Sensation*. The eye, Deleuze wrote, affects our senses. The idea to touch without real touching is interesting. I wanted to report on the roughness of the material without feeling its physically. I ended up scanning two paintings, cutting oblique lines as if I had put them in a paper shredder, and inverting the images. The result parasitizes the reading of the work and increases the feeling of a volume.

In other pieces, I worked on the pathology affecting tactility. I somehow consider painting as a disease, in the sense that it contaminates a surface. 'Hypoesthesia' and 'hyperesthesia' respectively mean weakened sensitivity/tactility and an increased sensitivity/tactility. The two pieces I produced in the end are the result of the aggression of the material as a surface.

FL: How do you feel about tactility in the contemporary and (in what way) does this inspire your work?

MB: In our present time, the need for touching seems to fade, because of a digital omnipresence. Data are dematerialized, things appear to us through a screen. A computer or a tablet is cold and smooth, and tends to make us lose awareness of the sensation of touching and feeling. In the end, my practice remains 'low-tech'. I keep a distance from new technologies. Indeed, if I sometimes work on a computer, I have to systematically go through the work of matter, and to manipulate, grind the object in order to give it its unique character.

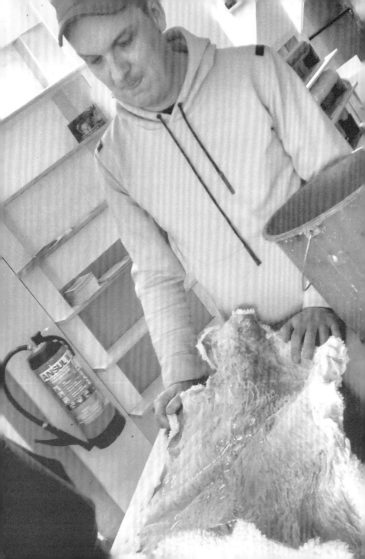

LIEVEN DE BOECK

"You can show more by leaving things out."

Lieven De Boeck in interview with
Brigitte Sloothaak en Sanneke Huisman

Clean is the face of rationalization and modernity; almost leading up to
a futuristic, collective hosophobia. White can be considered the colour
of the cultural elite, of high culture, of the divine on earth. Standardization
in language or building can be considered the best of man. In the craving
for and pleasure of cleaning and order, our push to purify might actually
be inspired by aesthetic motivations, rather than anything else. Could we
accept this deeply cherished experiencing, and leave all cultural identifying
and judgments aside?

FL: How did you initially feel about the request for a "concentrate / sample" of the tactile in your work and what was your first idea to process it into a piece?

LB: You can find tactility in my work mainly in its fragility. I often choose materials that question the representation of the idea. My work takes up a poetic position. The idea of a sample (or model) is a theme in my artist practice, as it includes already fragility. It is a test to see if something can work or if it fails. The failures are beautiful. On the other hand, I believe tactility can also exist in a thought. Tactility is present in the meaning of my works. These two ideas I wanted to include in the work produced at FMC.

FL: How did you start working at FMC?

LB: A couple of days before I started my residency I was washing a goatskin in my washing machine and added softener. The result was a weird object with a tactility that had completely changed. I decided to take this with me as a starting point for the project at Frans Masereel Centrum. After a first try-out of engraving it with a laser cutter, the skin was ruined. I bought a new skin and engraved a text in the leather part, in mirror image. As if it would have existed between the goat and its skin.

Tactility also often expresses itself better by putting it in front of its opposite, so I decided to work with the word nonsense. I found an empty plastic garbage bag in the studio at Frans Masereel Centrum. For me, this bag acts as one of the most sense-less objects in our contemporary western society; a garbage bag to put garbage in.

FL: How do you feel about tactility in the contemporary and (in what way) does this inspire your work?

LB: Tactility in the contemporary is challenged a lot these days. On the one hand in a rather negative way – by the over-presence of the image to produce ideas. But also – maybe in a positive way – through the discovery of new materials that can be 3D-printed. I believe tactility – in its idea and its material representation – stays a very powerful element to express contemporary positions in our society. In my practice as an artist, I early decided to never make a photo or video work; to rather work with objects that can be touched or, exactly, cannot been touched. Tactility as a main focus point.

FREDERIC GEURTS

"I can't make something in a void. I need a context. I like to interact with the surroundings. Both the spatial aspects and the significance of the space are important in this respect."

Sketching on paper allows enacting direct liberties of imagination. Front and back can optically be reimagined in a different spatial setting. Geurts works mostly with steel, building monumental, yet very fragile spatial outlines, in which the artist goes to the extreme in exploring the boundaries of gravity and the materiality of the constructions. By pushing the boundaries of the possible of the spatially set out confines on site, Geurts challenges the grid of our perceived reality. The perceived and the perceiver are constantly positioning themselves towards one another. The viewer is triggered to imagine the effective space the work holds in any other angle. Necessity and opportunity are in constant dialogue within this graphically set play of the spatial.

FL: How did you initially feel about the request for a "concentrate / sample" of the tactile in your work and what was your first idea to process it into a piece?

FG: I immediately loved the idea. Tactility is indeed something I feel related to. As a sculptor I am investigating if I can translate the qualities of a sketch into works in 3D. Especially the quality of the immediate, and the fact that hesitations and corrections are visible. I think tactility does come close to these qualities.

FL: How did you start working at FMC?

FG: A friend of mine, Peter Morrens, suggested to do some experiments with 'soft ground'. This is an etching technique where you use a soft varnish on the copper plate. Then you put thin paper on top whereon you make your drawing as usual. A bit like carbon paper, the lines remove the varnish. On these spots, the acid can reach the copper. The first trials proved this was a good idea. Preparing the copper plate takes a lot of time, but interestingly, the act of drawing is very immediate and the lines are incredibly tactile.

FL: How do you feel about tactility in the contemporary and (in what way) does this inspire your work?

FG: Difficult question. I think tactility has always

been present in art as something underlying every process of creation. I like to believe that the latest evolutions in contemporary art are showing more existential (and spiritual) approaches. Tactility is familiar to this. It's physical, it's about vulnerability and touches thereby existential issues.

ULRIKE MOHR

"Transformation does not just involve the
translation of wood into another medium,
it's about trees, branches, wooden rulers,
and metre rules becoming objects and
drawings in space – materialised memories –
material with a memory and a language
of its own – sounds that are overlaid
with their own echoes."

Ulrike Mohr taught herself how to make charcoal; either from natural or
cultural objects. While most artists traditionally use charcoal as a tool for
drawing, Mohr savours the aesthetic and conceptual riches of the decep-
tively modest material. While carbon emissions diffuse decay as a virus,
the clustering of carbon within objects can be perceived as the object-form
of imprints on grave clothes. Carbonized objects are like embalmed bodies.
They keep their original form, but with some shrinkage. All liquids, like
water are withdrawn from the object, leaving a stilled concentrate. The
objects become timeless.

FL: How did you initially feel about the request for a "concentrate / sample" of the tactile in your work and what was your first idea to process it into a piece?

UM: My first thoughts were: how to translate the concept of my process-based charcoal objects into tactile, print-related work? Working with charcoal represents a very particular form of concentration and compression to me. As if I hold my breath and concentrate, stop talking, stop breathing, hold still.

Despite its organic origins, charcoal resembles a black mineral – making its lightness all the more surprising when we hold a piece of it in our hands. It is crystalline and fragile, light as a feather and entirely light-absorbent. A materialized contradiction. Neither microorganisms nor animals can eat charcoal – the carbonized objects stay forever, they're beyond time's reach. On the other hand, charcoal is really fragile and ephemeral. I like working between those two antipodes, this is to me a state with potential for creativity. Charcoal doesn't only linger in different time cycles, it is always trying to balance the ordinary with the extraordinary.

FL: How did you start working at FMC?

UM: I started out with digitally laser cutting sheets of carbon paper. During the process, I became more interested in the production of this extremely thin paper. By chance I found a woody type of paper in the stock of Frans Masereel Centrum and carbonized it in a cookie box. I like to allow the material to take me somewhere. Like charcoal, the paper turned black and shrunk. The heat of the carbonization process models paper into an extremely light object, that looks somewhat like a topographical map. Depending on the surface, the colour becomes shiny or matte black. While working with carbonized paper, I was thinking about stories by Charles Fort, an American writer and researcher of anomalous phenomena, describing a rain of carbon papers falling from the sky. This is where the title 'Meteoritenpapier' comes from.

FL: How do you feel about tactility in the contemporary and (in what way) does this inspire your work?

UM: I like working with my hands black. What keeps me going is the sensory impressions while producing work, the smell, the fire, the sound of the carbonized works, the production process that is almost ritual. Ritual is a spatialization of the social in a way. In my exhibitions, the carbonized trees, branches, wooden rulers and other objects, become drawings in space – visible materialized memories.

THOMAS RENTMEISTER

"The sweet, the beautiful, suddenly turns
into the disgusting, the repressed
and the inappropriate."

Thomas Rentmeister works with industrially mass-produced domestic
materials. He often applies minimalist aesthetics or a poppy readymade-ness,
in order to reveal a physical ambivalence in our daily life. His works are
tangible within the abstraction they hold as their materials touch base with
our daily lives.

FL: How did you initially feel about the request for a "concentrate / sample" of the tactile in your work and what was your first idea to process it into a piece?

TR: Tactility is fundamental and recurring in my sculptural work. Recently, I produced soft ground etchings that made the connection between the printing process and the second-hand white underwear I had used in my sculptures before. The structure of the fabric was pressed onto a soft ground printing plate. This partially removed the varnish and let the acids erode the etching plate. The result was a 1:1 scale print with a very formal and abstract look-and-feel. But if you are aware of the origin of its motive – a garment, that once had been worn by a person – you still feel the spirit of this unknown person, though in a highly diluted way. With the residency that proceeded this exhibition, I wanted to advance with this project by adding a new component to it.

FL: How did you start working at FMC?

TR: In dialogue with Ivan Durt, the master printer at Frans Masereel Centrum, I decided to use digital technology to extend the etching practice I was already working on. We high-end scanned a piece of underwear. The large scale print of the textile structure was transferred through a chemical process onto a big copper plate. In the acid bath a beautiful relief of the texture emerged. The print itself had a certain blurring and blotchiness, caused by the higher quantity of production steps, the digital editing and the enlargement. In the beginning I wasn't sure if I liked it, until I decided to accept those inaccuracies as a new potential of the work.

FL: How do you feel about tactility in the contemporary and (in what way) does this inspire your work?

TR: It's good to write and think about tactility in art, but as an artist you primarily have to try it out by playing around with materials, and figuring out new ways of approach. Thinking by doing, in a way. This reminds me of the famous sentence by Joseph Beuys: *"Ich denke sowieso mit dem Knie"*, which he put on a postcard in 1977. I interpret this statement as a pleading for practical and physical experience. Especially in times when our life in the 'real world' is increasingly replaced by internet activities and digital experience, tactility is a kind of endangered species, that deserves protection.

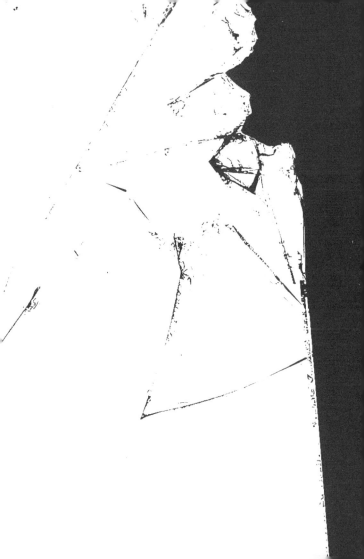

Lars Bang Larsen
TRACING CIRCLES
WITH OTHER CENTRES
Notes on print
and the materiality
of affect

'Typographic Man', wrote Marshall McLuhan in *The Gutenberg Galaxy* (1962), spawned from the invention of movable type. This was a technology that augured a new horizon for consciousness, but one characterized, however, by the repressive effects of a hierarchy of the senses with sight at the top — something that came to dominate the visible world through central perspective. As an alternative, McLuhan praised the simultaneous, tactile and lateral modes of communication brought about by the electronic age and the connectivity of the mid-20th century 'global village.'[1]

The fact that some artists today turn towards graphics can perhaps be better understood by rewinding the path of media evolution that McLuhan outlined in his futuristic progressivism. This is the return of a cutting and printing artistic subject who works physically with traces, differences, *caesura*. Because our life environment has become so abstract — 'immaterial' is the not entirely unproblematic term for this state of affairs — there is an understandable desire for that which is not mediated through digital media or conceived as readily transferable information; for something uncorrupted by flows of bits, money and images, something that the shadows of the real can fall upon.[2]

However, for all the directness and physicality involved in the techniques of letterpress, linocutting, woodcutting and so on, opacity and indirectness quickly enter the picture again. There is no reason to assume that contemporary printing artists have forgotten about the relativity of artistic media and institutional theories of the art concept, or that they choose to be ignorant about the mediated nature of the visual world in which we live. Their work is not a subversion of totalizing notions of contemporary 'complexity' in favour of an ethical simplicity of craftsmanship and visual one-to-one-ness. Instead they represent post-media practices that cannot be absorbed by a traditionalist discourse on the graphic arts or by any metaphysics of presence: echoing images, concepts, technologies and historical events that separate the graphic print from the humanism that it once expressed, they in this way form a reflexive return to the graphic surface.

The humanism (or anthropocentrism) of the graphic media comes down to mid-20th century use of graphic art as a vehicle for political messages or religious and existential myths. In post-WWII graphics — spanning the existential 1950s, the countercultural 1960s, and the political 1970s — it was understood that the printed art work was an Ariadne's thread out of barbarism. Also the sites of the graphic arts differed from the museum. Graphics were on the one hand associated with the intimate space of printed media — the book and the periodical — and as such with affordable art objects for working class or middle-class art consumption; and on the other hand they evoked the indexical aesthetics linked to the handout, the union poster, and direct action in the street — in short, popular and instrumental art forms that keep it real and depart from painting and sculpture as artistic modernity's canonized sensorium. When artists today return to such artistic media it has something to do with the myths and mobilizations of which these media used to be the visual face, but also with the fact that prints cannot be reconciled with our contemporary culture. They embody a return to artistic media that resist expansion and easy exchange.[3]

Because graphic media are essentially reproducible — and are, in fact, mass media in their own right — they don't form the symmetrical opposition to the endless circulation of digitally processed images that the unique art work would. Instead the image sequence formed by the graphically reproduced image manifest singularity in reproduction: a singularity of glitches and displacements that make one print different from the other. A copy is not a copy is not a copy...

From the point of view of recent artistic development, graphics obviously distinguish themselves from what can be called an entrepreneurial approach to art. The print is a hands-on affair: it cannot be 'managed', and it doesn't demand a division of labour with a view to optimizing production, as is the case with the highly operational artist's studio. Instead the print typically owes its existence to the direct artistic agency of the artist. Graphic art also distinguishes itself, in a more circumscribed way, from what has been called the social turn. In the 1990s, the social turn gave visual art a new lease of life at a point when it had otherwise been declared dead (along with the avant-garde, the novel, the human being, the author, etc.). The idea of the social contradicted the demonization of reality and presence in much of the work of the '80s: no longer something remote, academic and monumental, art became a situation or a process. A work was now a club, a bar, a meal, a cinema, a hang-out, a dance floor, a game of football or a piece of furniture. The sole author and the contemplative beholder were atomized in works that called for togetherness, and were often created by collectives or self-organized entities. The art institution started to reflect on itself as a critical space, and exhibition formats opened up in turn. Art took place anywhere – in front of a video camera, on an answering machine, in the urban space. Everyday life

ESSAY #1

became meaningful again, even a refuge from late capitalism, through a kind of social concretism that flirted with forms of presence from the distance of the developing digital media and the proliferating art media and institutional networks. Unlike this social concretism, the print — however concrete this may also be — is already an artistic sign. It is spatially removed from the social, too, in so far as an artist produced it in and for sites for artistic production and presentation.[4]

Importantly — and this is what I want to propose as another point where the tradition of printing impinges on contemporary art and theory — importantly, the poor, elementary nature of the print is also a way of grasping the presence of the non-human; forces that (to paraphrase McLuhan) work us over as humans. In this way the print is an aporia or meeting place of the human and the non-human. The non-human can be understood in terms of depictions of threats to freedom. Think of the posters of the May '68 Paris uprising, with their images of violent repression (riot police), abstract power (capital) and conformity (flocks of sheep).[5] As a propaganda tool and as an educator, the print has often carried images of disasters that prey on our humanity, from the bomb to unemployment, imperialism and sexism, and of course of whichever human agency might counteract them: unity, equality, emancipation, revolution.

Structurally, printing techniques often bear witness to the will of the material vis-à-vis intention: the wood and the stone resist and re-direct ever so slightly the carving tools, the rings of the wood re-appear in the print, the light reflects in the opacity of the ink... In the modernist print, *the ground* is often integrated in the figure; not in terms of background or middle ground, but as the industrially fabricated ground — paper, fabric — that carries and absorbs the humanly-artistically created figure.

Strung out between the human and the non-human, mass production and direct agency, craft and technology, the print is the art form that cannot hide its relations of production. This is the other side of its materiality. The painter can make the brush strokes invisible, and you cannot necessarily tell whether the sculpture is made with chisel or drill. The magic of photography is that it operates faster than the eye — not to mention the possibilities for post-production offered by the digital technologies. But the mark of the print remains the cut that separates black from white: human, and yet below the human.

The Materiality of Affect

Materiality can be defined in terms of relations of production. Experience always has a social body: to Marx, it is the decision-making processes that produce culture. These form the basis that conditions the social, legal, intellectual and political superstructure of a society, to which certain forms of social consciousness correspond. "It isn't human consciousness that determines their existence, but their social existence that determines their consciousness," Marx wrote.[6] In this way, when we look around the built environments in which we live and work there are few objects that aren't the result of somebody having brought them into existence.

To Marx, the totality of the relations of production was 19th century industrialism and the future it augured. The post-industrial economies of our time, on the other hand, tend to turn Marx's model of base-superstructure upside down. A significant part of today's economies of signs, images and creativity play themselves out in the superstructure through the processing and mediation of information, maintenance of legal and administrative apparatuses, the production of software and business concepts, and so on. Here superstructure has become more than mere ideology. Instead it is where power resides and produces entanglements between material and immaterial forms of production.

The work of Søren Andreasen offers us a way to connect the discussion of production to the problematic of the meeting between the human and the non-human that takes place in the print. In his linocuts Andreasen depicts almost-formed entities that evoke the non-human found at the level of plasma, molecules and dark matter. The reality principle that is his point of departure is the incomprehensible spasms of the nervous system that distort perception and prevent us from experiencing something other than the human world. In an essay from 2010, "Den ligeglade: Angsten for ikke at kunne begribe Det Almene" ('The Indifferent One: the anxiety of being incapable of understanding the common good'), Andreasen connects the languages of a materialism of human struggles and an organismic materialism by employing the Marxian concept of alienation to which he adds a Surrealist twist of paranoia and distortion:

Affect is the site of alienation. It is in affect that alienation is generated. The experience of the surrounding world replaces the materiality of the surrounding world, and becomes a place for the production of the nausea and of those fantasies that constitute the ontology of the alienated subject. It is a condition that thus stands in an incomprehensible and indirect relation to the surrounding world, in that its basis is the affectation's space of effects, rather than the causality of affect. The surrounding world is treated in a similarly indirect manner by the alienated subject, whose acts are speculative, fabulating or paranoid. In this sense the alienated subject is paralysed. Apathetic. Incapable of direct action. Incapable of understanding The Common Good, which in an evil logic often becomes the concept that haunts the alienated subject, and that this enlightened and free human being has probably enlarged himself in a massive way. Of course.[7]

ESSAY #1

What is considered uncomfortable and paranoid has another status in art than it has psycho-gically and socially. Aesthetically speaking, such alienation or estrangement can become expressive and productive. But when the fragile connection between thinking and affect is disturbed or instrumentalized, affect can become a closure, as is the case when it becomes a mercantile operation or is coupled with defensive or chauvinistic political passions. An affirmation of affect that evades critical thinking is therefore philosophically, aesthetically and politically suspect, just as an affirmation of philosophy, aesthetics and politics that evades affect is insufficient.

One can perhaps put it in terms of Louis Althusser's notion of 'overdetermination', that is, a causality that overflows its origins to address the question of manifold causes. A situation is overdetermined when several influencing factors act to affect it, as a socio-historical reality: these multiple factors mix and re-combine to bring about events. This is a radicalization of dialectics, because the multiplicity of causes is never resolved in an *Aufhebung*, is never unified and rendered organic à la Hegel. Instead the dialectical nature of the conflict among multiple causes is preserved. Causality is of an essentially conflicting nature, comprising "political laws, religion, customs, habits, financial, commercial and economic regimes, the educational system, the arts, philosophy" — and, we can add, affects and intensities that work our humanity over.[8] As a result, consciousness no longer has only one centre, it is no longer to be found within a circle of circles: it now has "circles *with another centre than itself*."[9]

Affect is an irritation or a rubbing of subjectivity. To the artist Andrea Büttner, shame is an aesthetic feeling, a paradigm for the reception and production of images.

> Shame marks the threshold of visual represen-
> tation and might at the same time be impossible
> to represent. Shame determines what we show
> or what we hide, what we expose and what we
> veil. Shame is intimately related to exhibiting, to
> the gesture of showing, to aesthetic judgement,
> and to the norms and conventions according
> to which we judge and move in the art world.[10]

In this (art) world considered as a zone of shame, making woodcuts is "the most uncool thing" the artist could do — a strategic and deliberate embarrassment that can disturb the professional codes and subtexts through which power is mediated.[11] A refusal to play the game — or better, to change its stakes.

There must be a good reason that artists intro-duce negative feelings or conditions such as aliena-tion and shame as central to aesthetic judgment. In the arguments of Andreasen and Büttner, subjective discomfort is inextricably bound up with specific his-torical and discursive conditions — with existing social space. Discomfort doesn't stem from the artist's being a genius, a misfit, or another kind of trans-historical, radical subject, but rather from the subject's interaction with certain culturally given relations of symbolic production, such as the role of the author itself. We can discuss this cultural nervous system in terms of what we could call a materiality of affect.

The contemporary horizon for affective materiality is the dissipated being of globalization that is processed in networks and drifting scripts. A world that is mobilized by capital is an affective and hyper-distracted world, one characterized by nervousness and restlessness. Adorno and Horkheimer talked about *Zerstreuung* in their critique of the culture industry, whose products one is capable of consuming, even in a condition of distraction — or especially in this condition. Accordingly, in the global culture industry, signification tends to be operational rather than hermeneutic: instead of interpretation, what creates value is *impact*—the production of effects and affect in the consumer's nervous system.[12] Language becomes an infrastructure that prepares impact, a plasma that is conducive to exchangeable effects and affects.

Affect is the sensory perception, the expressive and emotional activities that comprise our subjectivity. It is an immediate mode of sensual response, characterized by an accompanying imaginative or rationalizing dimension; i.e. what we perceive as good or bad food, what music incites us to dance, the kind of art that arouses us, events that make us indignant, and so on. In the perspective of determined intensities that make up a new apparatus of notionally immaterial production, affect also describes our ability to produce and consume in ways in which we invest our desire and creativity — intentionally or not. This is what is called immaterial work and production, yet the effects are far from ethereal when disembodied intelligences claw into our bodies. This affective turn in late capitalism subverts existing notions of alienation: think of what Fredric Jameson called the waning of affect, arguing that the late capitalist world had converted everything into surface.[13] Instead, we are more likely witnessing an *increase* of affect and inhabiting somatic states of heightened preparedness.[14]

For Deleuze, intensity describes what is virtual if real. Intensities have no form, composition or structure, and therefore no meaning or value in themselves. They are part of our being as a creative desire, and they inhabit a mental space: they are remembered and imagined and they produce linguistic realities — conversation, narration, text. They are half-present, determining causes that manifest themselves in the affect of the body, where they are given physical reality in the actual event of sensation. The intensity is part of the extension of time and the body, but never equal to what is lived and experienced.

In a global culture industry, intensity is an acceleration and a dilation of subjectivity that is mediated with a view to having an affective impact and a memorable effect in paying bodies. It usually takes the form of 'miraculous' communication that aims at giving consumers a feeling of increasing and expanding their subjectivity, of *being more* through distraction. In this case it is an affirmative stimulus. In a Marxist perspective, affects don't only exist over and above the cultural order, but are embedded in our social existence. One could even, polemically, paraphrase Marx and claim that 'it isn't the affectivity of people that determines their existence, but their social existence that determines their affect.' In this sense, the fact that we don't have affect, affect has us, would mean something over and above the cliché of being overwhelmed by the power of our emotions; it would mean that we are overwhelmed by the power of the stimulus to which culture has accustomed us to respond through internalized responses to given intensities.

But of course, one would immediately have to modify such a claim. It isn't the case that affect is irreducibly determined by our social existence in a certain symbolic order. This brings us back not only to Althusser's concept of overdetermination but also to Deleuze and Guattari, who emphasize that our subjectivity 'leaks' in processes that remove us from our historical space, and with which we human beings — as living, thinking subjects — respond in different ways to our social existence. Consciously or unconsciously, we subjectify — unlearn, re-imagine, re-inscribe ourselves in — culture.

We are not only reified and manipulated cultural cattle.[15] Affect is creativity, life.

There is more to the story, then, than being irremediably located inside a culture that determines the patterns of affect through which we move. But there is also more to the story than Deleuze and Guattari's emphasis on affect as art's window to an outside of subjectivity and culture. In fact we should probably look for the politics of the print, and its connection to affect, elsewhere than in spatial concepts of inside and outside: instead we should consider its temporal aspects. This focus on the time of the print is to some extent counterintuitive inasmuch as it is obviously a static image, and given that the print — as discussed above — often has been used to represent a space: the autonomous space of emancipation, the space of the community, the space of the street, the space of faith, and so on. In its propagandistic variants the print has also typically been used to express positive emotions and affect that are, ideally, constants: political passions, engagement, indignation.

The temporal aspect of contemporary artists' work with the print is the point where the full complexity of print-making and its involvement with historical space is focused. The artistic analysis of affective materiality that we today encounter in the print is a cut in time. Or you could say that it has its own politics of time — a particular chronopolitics. The chronopolitics of the print is first of all the *delay*, understood as the artist's tarrying with primitive manual instruments, with the hard and yet resonant surfaces, and with analogue procedures of duplication where affect — alienation and shame, for instance — are recorded and dramatised. In this delay expressive reverberations are bound to density and matter as a time-space that is different from capital's smooth spheres of circulation. In the print, effects are slow and affect becomes tactile and palpable. Sceptical.

Another layer in the chronopolitics of the print is its untimeliness; the fact that it is an anachronistic medium. Giorgio Agamben writes in his essay "What is the contemporary?":

> Contemporariness is, then, a singular relationship with one's own time, which adheres to it and, at the same time, keeps a distance from it. More precisely, it is *that relationship with time that adheres to it through a disjunction and an ana-chronism*. Those who coincide too well with the epoch, those who are perfectly tied to it in every respect, are not contemporaries, precisely because they do not manage to see it; they are not able to firmly hold their gaze on it.[16]

The untimeliness of print is obvious to everybody who spends their waking hours hooked up to electronic devices. You cannot log in to a print — it isn't *connective* — but things that are bigger than ourselves create

LARS BANG LARSEN

delays and intervals in the world, make us stop and wonder, re-direct being.

Such untimeliness could be articulated in terms of media archaeology, defined by Siegfried Zielinski simply as not seeking the old in the new, but finding something new in the old: an experimental attitude that has as its aim "not to seek the old that is already past in the new, but to reveal the new, the surprising, in the old".[17] Thus the current state of what has come and gone can give dead media new life. One has to add, though, that to include the graphic techniques in a discourse on media archaeology would deconstruct media theory's view of a genealogy of 'technical hearing and seeing.' One would probably have to revisit the concept of technology, in the modern sense of the term as an apparatus that optimizes the capacities of the human sense organs, from the contemporary perspective in which it seems that the graphic techniques are located at the limit of technology.

Media archaeology emphasizes the medium of time itself. In the deep time of media, time is seen to be out of joint, but at the same time opened up again: uncertainly redirected. As Zielinski puts it,

> The problem of imagining media worlds that intervene, of analysing and developing them creatively, is less a matter of defining an appropriate framework for this than of allowing them to develop with and in time.[18]

The artistic analysis of the materiality of affect is not reason's unraveling and submission of what has been sensed, but an unconditional exchange with those zones and time-spaces of life where being is whirled around by intensities. Here notions of historical progress and *telos* become radically uncertain as affect is reconnected to thinking. The concepts and procedures that evaluate affect can also be seen as intensities, as creative and generative bodies unto themselves. In this way the print is a block of artistic affect and a blocking of determined intensities, a hinge between historical experience and possible as well as improbable futures.

P.S.

Marx's concept of production clearly belongs to what Agamben calls "the anthropological machine of humanism", in which the human being is the central and self-present agent.[19] But what if agency cannot be so neatly and irreducibly located in human agents? Marxism itself seems haunted by the possibility of non-human agency, the possibility that matter thinks and exhibits agency. As Lenin asked, what does the car know — of its own relations of production?

The most famous example of non-human agency in Marx is his dramatization of the commodity in *Capital*, in which the fetish, here in the form of a table, springs to life and attains an uncanny liveliness while the worker is reduced to passivity. "So far as a commodity is a value in use, there is nothing mysterious about it," Marx asserts.

But, so soon as it steps forth as a commodity, it is
changed into something transcendent. It not only
stands with its feet on the ground, but, in relation
to all other commodities, it stands on its head,
and evolves out of its wooden-brain grotesque
ideas, far more wonderful than "table-turning
ever was.[20]

With his analysis or allegory of the dancing table, Marx
points out that the useful object, when it is detached
from its relations of production and re-appears as
a commodity on a market, seems as if it is worth
something in itself — and thereby hides the fact that its
value is actually the result of work, of social processes.
The spiritualistic allegory becomes Marx's dramatization of the battle between the social truth of labour
and the lie of commodity value; between use value
and exchange value. In Marxist terminology, 'spectral'
is a term for all that is pseudo and non-substantial in
capitalist society, the ideological nemesis of, well, a
table-thumping materialism.

The rhetorical devices with which Marx evokes dancing tables with theological whims is what Jacques
Derrida calls his "sensuous imagination", his "phantas-
mopoetic or phantasmagoric" description.[21] According
to Adorno, writing in his *Aesthetic Theory* (1970), the
phantasmagoric is *that which effaces the traces of its
production*: a Marxist definition, to be sure. However
we can postulate that spiritualistic phantasmagoria

may even have something to tell us about materiality and production because it registers the micro-event: every mumble, every shake of the table, every movement of the medium become significant. In other words spiritualism may be called upon artistically to take part in an analysis of and a meditation on late capital's immaterial relations of production, precisely because spiritualism is concerned with strange, affective appearances. This is what spiritualists call *materialization*: a ghost manifests itself in a body, whether that body is a human medium or another apparatus, such as a table or ectoplasm, light phenonema, kinetic disturbance, etc.

This digression on Spiritualism may have less to do with printing that with the theoretical discussions above, and with speculating on whether one can deconstruct Marx with a view to extracting a non-human materialism from his own text that is manifestly concerned with a materialism of human struggle. But consider this: with his infamous signing and selling of blank print paper as a future authorization of graphic works, Salvador Dalí cynically enabled the increase of his production beyond the grave and thereby allowed him to keep up his glamorous lifestyle in the years before he died. This was at the cost of artistic control, to say the least, inasmuch as the artistic signature in principle was a carte blanche for whatever posterity would add to the signed paper, under (or literally, above) the name of Dalí. But by deliberately creating

LARS BANG LARSEN

a marketable delay in his oeuvre at the risk of a future inflation of his artistic signature, he placed a time bomb in the pantheon and alienated the art-historical logic of eternity.

Chronopolitics indeed.

Notes

1   This essay was originally published in the catalogue for the exhibition BBBKK that took place at Bergen Kunsthal in 2012. It has been edited for the present publication in 2016.

2   John Rajchman muses on the problematic of abstraction and the materiality of media: "What is then abstract? Today the question arises in relation to what is known as the "information" age. Two related postulates might be distinguished. The first says that information is independent of the material medium through which it is transmitted; the second says that simulation and reality come to the same thing. Thus one "abstracts" from material support and, by replicating processes, abstracts them from the particularities of their real existence; even "life" becomes only abstract information, which can be replicated and so made artificially. The two postulates of immateriality and irreality then combine in the great conceit of the info era: that electronic devices will abolish real or material space and time and transport us all into another abstract, bodiless "space" or "reality," consummating the triumph of silicon over carbon. By contrast in Deleuze one finds an abstraction concerned not with extracting information from things (as though the material world were so much clumsy hardware) but rather with finding within things the delicate, complicated abstract virtualities of other things. Such abstractions don't entail independence or transferability from material support and don't operate according to a logic of simulation. Inherent, rather, in materials, they presuppose the subsistence of connections that exceed the messages of a medium and ourselves as senders and receivers of them. (John Rajchman, "What is Abstraction?," in *Constructions* (Cambridge, Massachusetts 1998), p 73.)

3   Adorno and Horkheimer characterize the culture industry in terms of 'expanded reproduction' (T.W. Adorno and Max Horkheimer, *Oplysningens dialektik* (Copenhagen 1995), p.187), and Adorno begins his *Aesthetic Theory* with the admonition that "In many regards, expansion appears as contraction" (T.W. Adorno, *Aesthetic Theory* (London 1997 / 1970), p.1).

ESSAY #1

4   See also my article "The Long Nineties", *Frieze* 144, (January-February 2012).

5   Cf. Kugelberg and Vermés, eds., *Beauty is in the Street. A Visual Record of the May '68 Paris Uprising* (London 2011).

6   Karl Marx, *Preface to A Contribution to the Critique of Political Economy* (1859).The author accessed the online version: http://www.marxists.org/archive/ marx/works/1859/critique-pol-economy/preface.htm (accessed June 7, 2012).

7   Søren Andreasen, "Den ligeglade: Angsten for ikke at kunne begribe Det Almene", in Søren Andreasen and Christian Schmidt-Rasmussen, eds., *New Age*, exh. cat., (Copenhagen 2010), translation by me.

8   Louis Althusser, *For Marx* (London 1996 / 1965), p. 102. Cf. Alexander R. Galloway's discussion of Althusser in "The Computational Image of Organization: Nils Aall Barricelli", in Karen Beckman et. al., *Grey Room 46*, (2012), pp. 27-43.

9   Op. cit.

10 Andrea Büttner: *Perspectives on Shame and Art: Warhol, Sedgwick, Freud and Roth*. Unpublished Ph.D. diss. (Royal College of Art, London 2008), p.3.

11 Andrea Büttner in Gil Leung, "Artists at Work: Andrea Büttner", Afterall Online, 2010. The author accessed the online version: http://www.afterall.org/online/artists.at.workandreabttner (accessed June 7, 2012).

12 Cf. Scott Lash and Celia Lury, *Global Culture Industry* (Cambridge 2007).

13 Fredric Jameson, *Postmodernism, or, the Cultural Logic of Late Capitalism* (London 1991).

14 See also my essay "Spredt væren" (Aarhus, 2010).

15 This is Andreas Huyssen's phrase in *Twilight Memories* (London / New York 1995), p. 17.

16 Giorgio Agamben, "What Is the Contemporary?" in *What Is an Apparatus? And Other Essays* (Stanford, 2009 (2006-08)), p. 41.

17 Siegfried Zielinski, *Archäologie der Medie. Zur Tiefenzeit des technischen Hörens und Sehens* (Hamburg 20029, p. 12.

18 Op. cit., 314.

19 Agamben, p. 29

20 Marx: "The commodity fetish and its secrets" in *Capital. A critique of Political Economy*, First book. (London 1992-93 / 1867), p. 170.

21 Jacques Derrida, *Spectres of Marx* (London 2006 / 1993), pp. 183 and 199. With reference to Marxism, Bruno Latour writes that until recently materialism was the same as an idealistic critique: "Typically, for instance, it was possible to explain conceptual superstructures by means

of material infrastructures. Thus an appeal to a sound, table-thumping materialism seemed an *ideal* way to shatter the pretensions of those who tried to hide their brutal interests behind notions like morality, culture, religion, politics, or art. But that's precisely the point: it was an *ideal* and not a *material* way of making a point." (Bruno Latour, *Can We Get Our Materialism Back, Please?* Isis 98, University of Chicago Press (2007), p.138.)

MISS RISOGRAPH

Riso remains a mystery to me. We met recently in my new office and I have to confess that I was drawn to her yet very intimidated. She is one of those types that can work fast and precisely without anyone's help. She only needs you in the beginning, after that you could not be more redundant. We agreed to meet after one of her thousand print-a-day rush.

JP Hey Riso, glad you could make it . I guess it is hard to find a moment in such a busy week. So as not to waste your precious time, could you introduce yourself briefly?

R Oh please, don't worry, I am a really fast worker, actually one of the fastest on the market. Anyway, I was born in the mid-20th century in Japan. My dad and his friends, the Riso kagaku corporation, saw great potential in me and dedicated their lives to my education. As a fast and modern worker I was used very quickly. I have always wondered whether it was because I am one of the cheapest and waste less printing processes, or because I very much look like silkscreen. The nice thing is that I used to be required to work only in print shops, yet with the democratisation of my process,

Q & A WITH

I am more and more often used in personal offices and small studios. And I have to say that this is very exiting!

JP Very well then, I am looking forward to having you in my own office... But could you convince our readers of the greatness of your skills?

R Of course, In my opinion I am a sort of hybrid of different ancestors printing techniques merged into one. My user's image is scanned and transformed into a master page. The master sheet goes through a heating process that burns out the voids of the drawing and is then sent over to the toner through which the inks goes. The paper is sent through this toner thanks to a high speed rotating system, reproducing the image quickly and without waste. Nevertheless, it is not advisable to use me for a small amount of prints, I think I am truly economical if you have a lot to create. Another great thing about me is that my masters only have to be there at the beginning of the process. Once the print is launched they can go, sit and relax.
On the other hand, that makes me very lonely...
So beneath this strong and independent figure, I am a very lonely person.

JP I am sorry to hear that, but I guess that you are the physical embodiment of a new kind of workers.

MISS RISOGRAPH

Which reminds me, how do you feel about the post-digital printing era?

R   Aha, I am actually very much looking Miss Risograph forward to it. I am sure, or at least I hope,
that the next generation will be able to achieve
great things! I mean, for instance, using new inks
into my process, such as the puff ink used in
silkscreen, feels doable. Or maybe Riso engraving,
with a system of relief matrices! Or Riso 2D printing! ... Sorry I am kind of loosing my mind. I am
under too much pressure, I get overenthusiastic
about things! But in a nutshell, I am very optimistic
about my future, whether it be in materiality or in
new forms of print. I doubt I will ever be archaic!

JP I hope so too as it would be great to combine your
fast lossless processing with some new materiality!
I believe you will achieve brilliant prints! Thank you
for having us Riso.

Marieke Sonneveld
BEING TOUCHED

The hand is often the icon for touch. Yet touch is a full-body experience. Our clothes, the floor we walk on, the chairs we sit on, are touched, but moreover: they touch us. The hands are symbolic because they represent *active touch*: we reach out, touch objects and by moving them (caressing, lifting, swinging, squeezing), we experience their materiality (texture, weight, weight distribution, hardness). The rest of our body is more *passively touched*: the clothes we wear, the chairs we sit in, and so on, and we do not feel their materiality, but rather their pressure on our body, the tickle, the warming effect, or sometimes the pain. Also, in every physical interaction, both phenomena occur simultaneously: we touch, and by that, we are touched. Touch is a full-body experience, literally inter-active. Thereby, touch gives us the feeling of *being in* control, exploring and manipulating the world around us, and at the same time it makes us vulnerable: it is through being touched that we can be irritated, harmed, or even destroyed. Hence the song: "Sticks and stones may break my bones, but words don't bother me".

Nevertheless, let's start with the hands, to understand the meaning of touch. Shaking hands is more than a brief ritual to say hello. It is an opportunity we

MARIEKE SONNEVELD

have to literally get in touch with the other. To feel how the other feels, and to experience how it is to move together. In this brief encounter we understand if that other is to be trusted or 'slick', is empathic or distant, is dominant, submissive or cooperative, full of energy or depressed, etc. In brief: to assess whether we want to stay in touch or not. That is: if we pay attention to it. An overarching concept to describe this phenomenon is 'body language'. When interacting with us, objects have a body language of their own. In a way, objects become animated: with skin, bones and muscles. And in touch, we do not really make a difference whether the object we are in touch with is actually alive or not: it is touching us, and thereby has affective meaning. Through their physicality, they express personality, intentions, and emotions, just like we do. We may not always be aware of it, but while being in the world, physically interacting with the world, we are continuously exploring what that world is 'communicating' to us on this affective level. We experience being loved or hated, being supported or let down, being challenged or patronised, and so on.

The sense of touch is all over our body. It is in our skin and in our muscles. We touch the world by experiencing how the world touches us, and by becoming aware of our body posture. The sense of touch is basically sensing our self: how we are touched, our body posture and the muscle force we are exerting.

NOTE #1

Objects invite us through their tactual properties to behave in a specific way, which in turn makes us feel in a specific way about our self. A wine glass will make us feel elegant, because of the delicate, refined posture of the hand, and the awareness that we have to be careful; the glass is vulnerable, so our movements become delicate. Whereas a beer glass will make us feel tough, because it is tough itself, and the way it has to be hold is tough: a strong grip involving the whole hand making a fist. Also, no need to be careful, it won't break that easily. And we might end up thinking, "same for me".

Touch defines the border between our self and the world. Touch defines the encounter between these two. Being in con-tact, means 'with touch'.

However, this border is fluid. Next to being *in touch* with objects, we are able to extend our bodies through objects, to make them become part of us. We touch the world, not only at the end of our body, but also at the end of our pen, our tennis racket, through the wheels of our bicycle, etc. We feel, experience the world *through* these objects, they become tactually transparent. Just like your phone disappears when you are in a call, and the chair you are sitting in disappears when watching a movie. It is a great talent of objects to be able to disappear, and impossible to ignore when they don't. We can not have a conversation while sitting at a tilting table: we fix it. Objects that keep asking for our attention become irritating. Also, next to designing for pleasure, designing for tactual transparency is a challenge. One should chose for the one or the other. Think of condoms: some are designed to minimize the irritation: to 'feel through', others are designed from a positive approach and to actually have an active role in the love play: they stimulate, add new sensations, etc.

Our daily life is not only about interactions 'here and now'; it is about the development of these interactions over time, resulting in the kind of relationships we build together. Affection is not only about warmness, softness and tenderness. Positive affective relationships are not only characterized by the comfort zone: care and support, but also about pushing the boundaries of it, by challenging each other, creating space for growth, and by doing this with humor. The same goes for our relationships with objects.

Positive interactions may result in friendships, such as our relationship with our reliable, relentless bicycle, our enthusiastic running shoes or our welcoming armchair. Negative relationships may develop into animosities, like the ones we have with the nagging newspaper that always needs more support to stay in shape than we can offer, or with the stubborn front door key that needs a special treatment before it gives in. And finally, mixed experiences may result in maybe the most interesting: the love-hate relationships. Like we may have with our cars, skateboards and other sports gear: demanding objects that, once tamed, provide great experiences of flow, of being a team together.

NOTE #1

So what? Why would we care about these aspects of touch? We chose the objects we surround our self with. By becoming aware of their body language, of the way they affect us, we are able to shape to a large extend the affective meaning of the world we live in.

Explore the physical world you created around you, and ask yourself: does this world love me? Support me? Challenge me? Does it meet my affective needs? And if the answer is no, reach out for the objects that have the power to create the affective experiences you are longing for, and invest in a good relationship with these objects.

MISS SILKSCREEN

Meeting silkscreen in a squat was a unique experience. It felt pretty unusual to see this icon of pop art used by young alternative kids. Silkscreen seemed to be so popular, so perfect, so smart as a technique of reproduction but it looked as if she wanted to be rebellious and make a statement by giving herself to young punks. And somehow she did prove how unexpected she could be.

JP Hey Silkscreen, good to see you again. Could you tell us a little about yourself ?

S   Hey! Yeah, good to see you too. Well... It's always hard to be true when talking about oneself, but I will try. I was sort of reborn at the beginning of the 20th century, after many attempts in China that did not work that well. And I became instantly famous. My teen years were great. I was used by everyone, from advertisers to rebellious alternative punks and even by famous artists! I mean, can you ask for more? I really nailed my 15 minutes of fame. As for now, well, I am still very busy. With the D.I.Y trend, I have become a sort of nostalgic Icon of print.

JP All right then. Could you explain this fantastic pro-

Q & A WITH

cess that made you world famous ?

S   Well unlike the digital printing process, I am a
    very hands-on technique. My masters really have
    to get in close contact with me. I am quite a piece
    of work too! And I am slow and expensive. And
    yet one of the greatest. First things first, you have
    to make a bitmap file that will be printed as a sten-
    cil image on a screen. The screen itself has to go
    through a specific chemical process to allow the
    image to be turned into a mesh. Once the frame is
    ready, my masters can use a wide range of inks and
    supports. I mean I can print puffed ink on textile,
    metallic ink on paper and so on and so forth...
    The act of printing is a whole ceremony. You have to
    apply ink to my screen and press it carefully so the
    ink is evenly spread onto the mesh and goes through
    it. The drying process himself is rather quick and
    allows for a fast reproduction of the image.

JP I see! I think we got all the information needed here.
    But to go a little further... how would you say you
    relate to the post digital era of print?

S   We'll have to say that digital print is more of an
    advantage for me. Indeed with the arrival of digital
    software such as photoshop it is much easier to
    create bitmap files. And I am willing to mix with
    inkjet printers as I think it is rather interesting to

MISS SILKSCREEN

have let's say a silkscreen image over a printed picture! And as I mentioned before, I am now popular
because I am steeped in nostalgia. It almost feels
like digital printing made me even more popular
than before, although in a different way. So yeah,
I do have great faith in the future... Or at least in
my future.

Alessandro Ludovico
THE TOUCHING CHARM OF PRINT

Printed media have a highly consolidated visual infra-structure. But their (preponderant) visual part has been wrongly considered as coinciding with their whole. That is why they have been recently massively translated into another universal medium (the digital) through a direct process. What is missing, much more than nos-talgia, is a small perceptual universe that is instinctually unfolded every time the physical medium is used, while it is misdirected if not negated in its new screen-based embodiment.

Screen touch vs. print tactility

There is a recurring comparison in the media between the convenience of using printed content in digital form versus its traditional paper format. A published work in a computer file format has a series of promoted qualities: lightness and hence portability, speed in accessing it, its (near) instant ability to be searched, quantified, linked, cross-referenced and more in general "calculated," which makes it a terrifically tool-enforced version of the original work. But there is a constantly underesti-mated aspect: its "user experience", especially from a

ALESSANDRO LUDOVICO

perceptual perspective, which, paradoxically, turns out to be quite "deprived" compared to the classic printed publication. Digital content uses primarily one sense: sight. Excluding taste, of course, to start there is an absence of any specific smell. Hearing may or may not be involved, and when it is, it usually appears in two different ways: print experience simulation (typically a sound sample of turning pages), and alert sounds, which are unspecific, so not contextualised to the reading experience. In fact, they belong to the more general digital interface, being generally meant just to attract attention about some impeding fault or to warn for something about to happen. Sight, instead, is very involved, although the text appears always in the very same way, thanks to the retro-illuminated characteristic, which is meant to ensure readability anytime, anywhere.

In comparison, classic printed publications are using a much richer sensorial environment, providing inputs for multiple sensory modalities.

Again excluding taste, smell is quite directly involved in the composition and age of both paper and ink, indirectly giving specific information about the text, also because it varies a lot, even within the same olfaction domain (old books smell in an ample different degrees of dust and mould, depending on their exposure to light, specific preserving environments, composition of paper and inks, etc.). Hearing is mainly about the physical manipulation of the book, which implies the sound of bending and closing the, usually thicker, cover, which is quite different from flipping or turning the pages. Very importantly, each time we turn a page, the resulting sound is slightly different, and not really quite the same as it is in simulated digital environments. Sight, eventually, also varies extensively, print being front-illuminated and therefore depending on very different (natural or artificial) lighting conditions, with all their degrees, technologies and filters involved.

And finally touch, and thus tactility, is just reinforcing this comparison. In the digital realm we have a merely functional and decontextualised touch: if we still use mouse or trackpad "prosthetics", our fingers are functionally used for clicking, swiping, or tapping in the very same way for all the different types of content, but in a standardised universal modality, which, again, cannot be conceptually unplugged from the inescapable design of digital interfaces. In the digital realm our fingertips are simply annihilated, even if they possess the highest concentration of touch receptors and thermoreceptors of all the areas of the human skin, aside from our genital parts. From being extremely sensitive and "broadband" input sources for our body they become neutral machine-oriented prosthetics.

In traditional print tactility gives information on different levels, and the process of paper selection is, in fact, still an important part of quality publishers' work. It gives information about colour (sight), texture

ALESSANDRO LUDOVICO

(touch) and odour (smell) that is, possibly. consistent with the whole of the work. If we are already familiar with a book, the texture of its cover unawarely gives us information about its content (confirming what we are about to read) even before we open it, and eventually we would be able to recognise certain books while being blindfolded. Every added element (lamination of any type, hollow punches, special inks) is not just an additional piece of information, but a further experience that is perceived both by sight and touch. Our senses are constructed to have a "very large bandwidth", and "sense" is derived from the Latin word "sensus" that, in this respect, means 'faculty of feeling', which is all but mechanical. Tactility, as any other sense, is about perceiving differences, and the more differences we are trained to perceive, the more we learn and the more we are able to perceive, in a virtuous endless circle. ?

On the other side, even state of the art digital publications are still a "simulation" of the printed ones (like the classic pdf standard), in a quite ambiguous trajectory. They mimic the structure and conventions of print, adapting them to the needed digital parameters, but they probably fail in re-creating a similar experience, and trying to appeal to sight as much as possible, including, for example, the visually compelling fast zooming (in and out) abilities. The screen has uniquely flexible qualities, but it can't effectively render three-dimensional space if not through a simulation which our senses know is flattened, in any case. It is how French researcher Émeline Brulé defines the digital simulation of print: "mimetism."

The material space of information

How many things do we physically "touch", establishing an enriched relationship with them? Not too many – but screens and printed materials are surely among them. More generally, materiality has its own space of information, which is very different from the immaterial one. The three-dimensional space of materiality is essential in locating, estimating and recognising cultural objects. But there is more. Since the senses are involved, we often make an emotional investment in these objects and we don't want to lose this investment in the inappreciable, enormous size of the digital space, experienced through a small bi-dimensional screen. Digital publications, being prone to the screen, would have to cope with this aspect of their own nature, but, in turn, they would also exploit their unique ability of hosting infinitely reprogrammable and infinitely transmittable content. Instead of simulating the (unsurpassed) print "interface", which has been gloriously established and refined since more than five centuries, they would build on the ability to instantly create, combine and calculate content, trying to accomplish an intimacy between writer and reader similar to the one that McLuhan attributes to printed materials. And, if properly handled, tactility could play a fundamental role in this process, even if there is no simple equation to fill the gap between the machine and our fingertips. In robotics, for example, the still primitive "tactile sensors" are devices measuring information derived from physical interaction with their environment, but they are generally modelled after the biological sense of cutaneous touch, and they are definitely uncertain, for example, when it comes to sensing "pain." In digital publications tactility would be enhanced in a proper way, avoiding clumsy simulations, and appealing instead to our nerve endings in a direct way, maybe through interconnected new artificial materials. They would provide new information to the screen reader, being eventually able to materially assume a decent number of textures or "states" that were unperceived before, appropriately reflecting their possibly direct and instinctual relationship with the content. Then, the two different worlds would begin to be comparable, and even an hypothetical hybrid between them could begin to be conceived. It would be in direct relationship with our senses, but simultaneously be able to reflect both the stability of the printed page and the perennial dance of information inour digital world.

Q & A WITH

MISTER ETCHING

I met Etch a few years ago in the dark corner of a printing shop. He was standing straight and tall, a bit rusty but still very elegant. He was quite intimidating as he seemed to be a bit academic and not exactly cool. But I did overcome my shyness and we had a nice conversation.

JP Good evening, Sir. How are you today?

E So far so good, but I won't be able do stay too long tonight… I don't want my chemicals to dry too fast as it would slow my work and disturb my master.

JP All right then. Could you please introduce yourself briefly?

E Be glad to. My name is Etching, Etch if you will. I was born in the Middle ages. My parents were trying to find a printing technique that would reproduce drawings on paper. I was loved beyond words and had a nice childhood. My masters were always very grateful and I have to say with some pride, that I did bring fame to quite a few artists, such as my friend David Hockney. I am now still used by drawing masters, yet with the arrival of digital printing machines I have become a little obsolete.

Q & A WITH

JP Could you explain how you work?

E Well, unlike in digital printing, I am in direct
contact with my user. The artist handling me has
to engrave my body directly with a thin metal nee-
dle. The most painful part of this intaglio process
is that I have to be covered in acid or mordant to
soften my skin and make it smooth enough to be
marked. Once washed and lusted I am covered
with ink and sent to a high pressure printing press.
I have to confess that it is the most pleasant part
of the process. The contact of my body with the
paper, both pressed against each other while the
ink is being released… It's just heavenly. And the
most rewarding aspect of it is that once the pain
of engraving is over, the pleasure of printing can
be repeated indefinitely, as long as there is ink and
paper at hand.

JP Very exiting, it sounds like you value your physical
interaction with other material more than anything…
So, how do you see yourself within what they call
the post-digital era of printing? Would you say that
you are scared of becoming antiquated? But maybe
you like nostalgia. Do you ?

E Funny you ask. I've just had a discussion with
a letterpress from my workshop, and unlike
him, I have a lot of faith in myself. I believe that

MR ETCHING

even in an all-digital-printing era, drawing masters as well as amateurs will strive for a hands-on approach to printing. My fellow friend, Epson stylus 1500 W, never gets truly touched by his user, while I am really worked on by my user's hands. I think this is this interaction that makes me so likeable even though I am a slow and expensive worker. You know, there is this tension in my working process... one can fail, not control his hands, make mistakes... This chance encounter is what somehow makes me so special. I turn the fear of making mistakes into something mysterious and exciting that only reveals itself at the end of the whole printing process. And this, I think, digital printers don't have. They are so precise, so much in control, but so imperfect in their own perfection.

JP I am glad to hear that you have faith, Etch! We really hope to see you among us in the next printing decade.

Esther Krop
TACTILITY (= SENSE OF REALITY) IN PAPER PUBLICATIONS

Tactility (or how something feels: smooth, soft, rough, etc.) is a concept which plays a big role in paper publications at the moment. Through the sense of touch we orient ourselves and make contact with our physical environment. Apart from visual and auditory possibilities, digital media can be quite limited and one dimensional when it comes to tactile sense. What you feel while using a computer or smartphone is not much more than the keys of a keyboard or the glass of the screen, which may give off small vibrations. And although there are developments which aim to focus on tactile senses by using haptic feedback, these techniques are still in their early stages.

Out of the five senses, 'seeing', 'hearing', 'tasting', 'smelling' and 'feeling', digital media only fully address 'seeing' and 'hearing'. So, we miss a part of reality, because 'tasting', 'smelling' and 'feeling' are not called upon. This explains, as I see it, the need for paper and print techniques that highlight the tactile senses. 'Feeling' is missing in the digital world, and it is something we also want to experience, because it is, in fact, part of our perception. 'Smelling' and 'tasting' we do elsewhere, but for 'feeling' there is a big opportunity in print. With a history of a thousand years and endless modes of expression, paper and print are fantastic tools for discovering reality and imagination through stimulating the tactile senses. With tactile printing you can diversify yourself, not just from the computer screen, but also from other (bulk)publications. Starting from my field expertise as a paper adviser, I will outline some remarkable developments on the case of tactility:

Business cards: 'Dick, dicker, am dicksten?'

The business card: a simple card the size of a credit card featuring your contact details, that you give to a business relation so that they might remember you. Why should this be more than an unnoticeable carrier of information? But still you see the desire for thicker cards, even up to half a centimeter. Not very practical, but it makes an impression. The German paper supplier Metapaper has launched a campaign called 'Dick, Dicker, Am Dicksten' for a kind of paper that is especially developed to print thick business cards on a digital printing press. 'Multiloft' is the name of the paper, which consists of a top layer that can be printed on digitally and which can be glued onto one or more colored layers of cardboard on the inside. The glue has already been applied to the paper and cardboard and can go through the printer as it is – making the paper easy to handle. The American company moo.com offers the same type of cards with the slogan 'A difference you can truly feel: everyone who receives one will experience a quality and weight like no other card.' Weight is thus also a keyword when it comes to tactility. Another example is a beautifully colored paper called 'Colorplan'. Colorplan is available in 50 colors and 8 different weights (up till 700 g/m^2). Different layers of this paper can be glued together; This is called 'duplexing'. This technique is used often for business cards, of which the front side has a different color than the back side. The trend of using business cards that are overweight has also not remained unnoticed by the online printing press Drukwerkdeal.nl. They offer, among other things, aluminum business cards of 0,4 mm (1080 g/m^2).

Revival of the 'old' printing techniques
The recent revival of 'old' printing techniques such as letterpress (printing press) and riso print (stencil printing) is to me an indication that tactility plays a big role in distinguishing between forms of print today. Letterpress is suddenly hip again, which fits in with the broader social desire for authenticity and purity. Letterpress is a first-rate tactile printing technique, because of the laborious process: the use of lead type and cliches, heavy presses and ink that sticks to the palette-knives. It is possible to produce a large amount of copies with letterpress at a printing office specialized in foil press,

or you can do it yourself in a small letterpress studio. In relief printing the paper will show lasting, be it minute marks. This being as typical for the technique as the overflow of ink around the edges of the printed typeface was avoided because looking old-fashioned in the time offset came up. Today the 'imprint' or 'embossment' is seen as a fine and haptic quality to be recognized by the sensitive. The paper suppliers have followed this trend by producing specific letterpress papers containing a large percentage of cotton, which is very suitable for an effective and deep embossing. For example, the paper manufacturer Gmund from Germany makes 'Gmund Cotton', a 100% cotton paper with a thickness up to as much as 900 grams. Gmund's tagline for the product is 'pure cotton, soft and gentle, elegant and superlatively thick. Feeling is believing!' With letterpress, you actually hold something in your hands, the whole process requires a hands-on mentality. Risography, the old stencil printing from the '60 and '70, has seen a revival as well. Artists, designers and independent publishers are experimenting with Riso. Risograph printing is an affordable technique for producing a small amount of copies. The Netherlands is home to riso specialists such as Knust in Nijmegen and the Charles Nypels Lab, part of the Jan van Eyck Academy. In 2014 The Charles Nypels Lab organized the first International RISO Expert Meeting. Riso ink on paper produces a very special, intense effect. The ink is absorbed by the paper and the color literally starts to vibrate. If you aren't careful, the ink can lead to stains or stick to your fingers. For Riso, only a rough (and bulky) types of paper are suitable. This adds to the raw, DIY, and non-pretentious vibe of the technique, which differs greatly from offset and the daily prints we see in everyday life.

Paper with a touch

You have to see and feel paper. This is the reason why I started De Monsterkamer, a physical database for paper which, for now, there is no digital equivalent of. Some suppliers have impressive websites, www. gfsmith.com or gmund.com for example, where you can get a fairly good look at the colors and textures of the paper they supply. The ability to feel the paper, however, is missing completely. Which would seem a significant ommision, no?

The last couple of years has seen a reduction in paper production, which results in a large amount of paper types not being available anymore. Yet, the field is still innovating, including innovations in special paper. Paper manufacturer Arjowiggins has just released a collection book weighing 3,5 kilos: The Paper Book shows their entire collection of creative paper on A4. The Arjowiggins collection contains multiple innovative types of paper with a special 'touch'. For example, 'Curious Touch' which offers a sensual, soft and rubberlike coating. Another example is 'Curious Matter', a paper covered with microscopic balls of potato starch, which gives it the feel of sand, or a soft kind of sand paper. The English paper manufacturer G.F Smith presented their entire paper collection in a big book as well, weighing 1,5 kilos and counting 403 pages. The book shows us 130 years of experience bundled up in beautiful paper, 45 brands and 5 different collections. This is the new way of showing paper. Paper is starting to get more and more into a niche, and collections are being displayed in exclusive books.

Paper with structure

When it comes to creating subtle surfaces, The Japanese are the masters. Japanese manufacturer and distributor Takeo has in its selection a range of paper with very fine structures. The last exhibition about paper from Takeo (which they have organized since 1965) had the suitable title and theme 'Subtle'. German manufacturer Gmund recently introduced 'Gmund Urban'. This collection contains paper with real cement, paper structured with wood nerves and with very delicate micro-embossings. "Introducing a fresh take on raw materials." It's back to basics, but more high tech. The simplest and cheapest way of giving print a special feel is by using a soft touch laminate. Laminate is something that can be added to every standard paper, and which has a very surprising effect.

Binding makes all the difference

How a book feels in your hand, makes a big difference

as to how you perceive it. Is it heavy or light, flexible or hard, thick or thin? Some designers make the mistake of choosing a rather stiff paper, with too many grams, because they are afraid 'it will shine through' in case they choose a lightweight paper. The result is a book in which the pages turn as if they were wooden shelves. The weight of a book – or even that of a business card, as we have seen before – is part of its tactility. To make a book lighter but still voluminous, one can use bulky paper. This is paper with more air inside. Sometimes a thick book might not seem as heavy as you thought once you pick it up. On the other hand, a machine coated paper can be used to make a book heavier, which can also add a certain charm. There are flexible ways of binding books, and ways that make it more stiff. Gold glue is flexible, PUR is stiff, and Hotmelt is something in between those two. A very popular binding method is the 'exposed sewing'. With this technique a bound book block is fixed with transparent glue. The book cover and the spine are left out, which has the advantage that the book is opening up easily. This book binding method gives the book an unfinished look, which might not be appreciated by every reader. There have been stories of publishers who received their books back, because the consumer thought there was a mistake in the printing process.

Tactility is in fact a subtle combination of material, weight, surface, printing and book binding method. Or did I forget something? Oh yes, the perceiver.

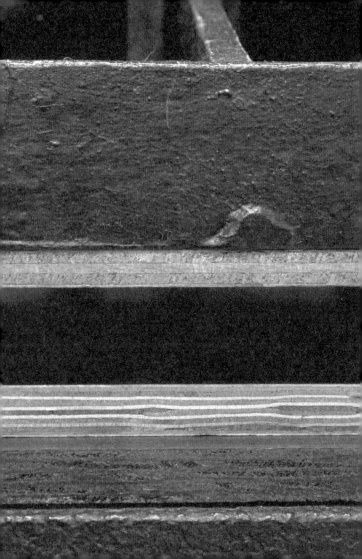

MISTER LINOCUT

Ah Lino... Such a beautiful character, and tender too!. I had the nicest encounter with him last year while I was doing a minor on printing. Completely overwhelmed by the imposing Etching and lithography, I did not notice Lino at first. Still Lino made a really modest, yet valuable entrance in my research. He was so friendly, so accessible and generous. And we are still very good friends.

JP Hi Lino, always good to spend time with you!
I would like to share my passion for you with my fellow readers. So would you be so kind as to tell us a bit more about yourself?

LC Well, I had, in some ways, some very shameful beginnings. Not that I was a shameful creation. It's more the way other people perceived me. My German family, Die Drucke, preferred to lie about my own nature in the beginning, pretending I was a form of woodcut. All this masquerade because I did not look that noble in their eyes... It was only in the 1950's that I gained a lot of respect in the art field with the help of my master Walter English Anderson. That was a life-changing experience and it helped me to stand for what I was and not something else looking like woodcut. I mean when

you are used by Pollock for instance, there is no
need to have doubts about who you are.

JP I could not agree with you more, my dear. You mentioned many times an affiliation to wood cut. Could
you actually explain it so we know a bit more about
your working process?

LC Indeed there are similarities between us. But let
me explain. The idea is that you work on my skin,
which is a very strong yet tender material made
of linseed oil, pine rosin, ground cork dust, wood
flour combined with minerals to bind all those
things together. And this is already different from
woodcut, I am tender and made of multiple materials, while he is rough and only made of wood.
Anyway... So my masters have to engrave their
images in my soft skin with chisels or gouges. And
then again, gouges are also used for woodcutting.
But because I am easier to engrave, my masters
can realise more set patterns. Once the image
is drawn I am covered with ink with a roller and
finally sent to meet the paper. This meeting sometimes happens in a printing press, but can even be
done manually. In this sense I am every accessible,
I can be used easily by non professionals at home.

JP Interesting. So do you think those D.I.Y abilities will
allow you to survive the post digital printing era?

MR. LINO CUT

LC Indeed, I very much think so. On the other hand,
   I also believe that I am not a technique that should
   be seen as being opposed to digital printing,
   but rather as one you can combine with. I truly
   think that there is a great collaborative potential.
   I very much see myself being applied over an
   inkjet printed image. And I have to confess that
   Riso triggers me a lot... So, no, to be honest, I look
   forward to the future rather than fear it.

JP Indeed, we should combine both forces to create
   new forms of print... Thank you for your time Lino,
   let's meet again soon!

Rik Peters
DO NOT TOUCH: THE PHENOMENOLOGY OF TACTILITY

It appears to be a trivial tautology that the visual arts are directed at the spectator's *visual* experience. Beauty is in the eye of the beholder: art is produced for the eyes and consumed through the eyes. But the practice of galleries and museums contradicts this formula: if visual art is an exclusively visual affair, why the ubiquitous 'do not touch' signs? The explicit and oft-repeated prohibition against touching is an appeal to suppress an urge that most spectators have: to feel the artwork's texture, to experience it not just visually, from a distance, but in skin-to-skin intimacy. Do not touch signs point to a fundamental property of visual art: it appeals to our sense of touch as much as to sight.

The model of traditional psychology, dating back at least to Aristotle, maintains that there are five senses: sight, hearing, touch, taste and smell. Each neatly separated from the others, each the receptor for a distinct domain of experience. This model has been out-of-date for quite a while. First, because it is impossible to reduce all of human experience to these five senses alone – consider the perception of heat, of hunger, or of balance: to which of the five headings do they belong? Second, the boundaries between the senses are far less distinct than we were told in elementary school. The intimate connection between taste and smell is the most obvious example, but there are many more: horror movies combine sound and vision to create an effect of suspense; culinary chefs know that the texture of a dish has a significant influence on its taste. Of these connections, perhaps the most prominent one is the link between seeing and feeling, vision and tactility.

We do not need to actually touch something to access its tactile qualities like texture, weight, smoothness or the motion of curves and planes. All these qualities are already apparent in the visual sensation, albeit in a weaker form than when we would actually touch the object. We 'feel' with our eyes, we 'see' tactile qualities: in this sense, all perception is synesthetic. The red colour of a wool carpet is always seen as a distinctly 'woolly red', even if spectral analysis shows that the wavelength of the colour is the exact same as the red of a smooth surface. We never see the colour detached from the texture in which it is embedded, and we never see a texture without 'feeling' it, if only virtually. A heap of autumn leaves does not transmit a neutral visual image, but suggests the feeling and sound produced by the cracking of dry leaves. These sensations are already given in the visual perception of the leaves. What is more: the visual perception invites us to touch the red carpet or the dry leaves, to let them fulfil the tactile promise they silently make to the spectator. Perception is not only synesthetic, it is also laden with meaning and promise: one sense suggesting another, pointing beyond itself, indicating the possible sensations, meanings and actions it might evoke. In this way, a visual sensation is always more than itself. This is the reason why certain paintings, sculptures or installations require a reminder to the spectator: do not touch, do not take up the tactile challenge this work presents to you.

For artists, this transcendence of sensation is an indispensable tool to create meaning. When encountering a canvas by Monet or Cézanne, we do not only see a collection of coloured patches in the shape of a landscape – it suggests sensations that we do not actually experience, but that are nevertheless virtually present in the visual givens. We know what the landscape will look like beyond the picture's frame; we also know what it would be like to walk through this landscape, to feel the lush grass touching our bare feet and to hear the rustling of leaves. This is not only because we have seen this kind of landscape before: the surrealist landscapes of Dalí or Max Ernst equally engender meanings beyond their direct givens – not in the last place the tactile suggestions. And even abstract images point beyond themselves: Lucio Fontana's canvases with holes and slashes are a particularly violent example of visual art emitting a tactile meaning.

RIK PETERS

How does the communication between the visual and tactile givens of experience come about? Following Maurice Merleau-Ponty, we can state that it is founded on a twofold unity: the unity of the body on the one hand, the unity of the world on the other.

The traditional five senses model treats the body as a machine with a number of independent sensors attached at various points. The impressions of these sensors are all communicated to some supposed central seat of consciousness that combines them to create a single representation of the world. This traditional picture, however, ignores the intimate complicity of the senses: they are not appendages of a machine to begin with, but functions of a living body. A living body that finds itself in situations, adopts attitudes towards its environment, and undertakes projects. The senses are the means by which the body can orient itself in the world – and this orientation is always primarily practical and motoric. When seeing, touching or hearing, we are scanning our environment for possible actions, for points of contact with the world. Every sensation is already endowed with sense and meaning, because it already provides a certain suggestion of motion to our body. Because sensation is rooted in the possible movements of the whole body, the boundaries between the senses are permeable: for example, the mere sight of a heap of dry autumn leaves suffices to suggest the feeling and sound of the leaves cracking, because it is not the *eyes* that see the leaves,

NOTE #4

but the *body* that sees it *through the eyes*.

Besides the unity of the body, the connection between the different senses is also due to the unity of the world. Although the five senses give different kinds of information, they all provide us with access to the same world. In a concert hall, one may hear and see a string quartet at the same time, but it is impossible to separate these sensations: we hear the string quartet playing on stage. The sound comes from the direction in which we are looking – there is no strict separation between the sensations of the eardrum and the images on the retina. So, too, with the red wool carpet: the carpet is a single object, which we happen to apprehend in different ways with different parts of our body. But it is no surprise that these qualities intermingle, that the red colour is infused with a woolly quality, even to a spectator who remains at a distance.

Of course, not every image has the same tactile power – only objects that send out a particularly forceful invitation to touch are provided with a sign saying 'do not touch'. In most cases, the tactile dimension is too subtle to charm the spectator into actually touching. Nevertheless, a tactile dimension is always present, in any work of 'visual' art, be it in two or three dimensions. The world presents itself to us through our body and its various channels that all work together to elicit a sense of meaning from the world. There is no meaning without tactility – and consequently, there would be no art without embodied spectators.

MISTER LITOGRAPHY

I never got to know lithography too well. We met two years ago during a graphic workshop. He was there, siting nonchalantly on a table. Despite his posture, he looked stately and somewhat elegant. I came to understand later that Mr Litho is a very heavy and edgy person, but he has gained a lot of respect from his peers. Everyone treats him respectively. So did I...

JP Good afternoon, Sir. Would you be so kind as to introduce yourself to our readers?

L I will. My dad, Alois Senefelder, was a poor German author and actor who needed a cheap and fast reproduction process to spread his writings around. This is how I happened to be brought into the world, at the end of the eighteenth century. From this quite limited action of printing text, I became famous thanks to my ability to reproduce drawings and other images with a very refined and tactile expression. Moreover, with the later birth of my cousin chromolithography, we got into the field of scientific imagery printing, which in my opinion is one of the most precise printing techniques. Nowadays printing techniques are clearly inspired by the way I operate. Offset lithography,

my grand-son, is doing a great job when it comes
to mass reproduction of books and magazines.
Yet, I am not sure he has my sensitivity. I will say
he is more effective then affective.

JP I could not agree more with what you said earlier
about scientific print, I myself collect them. Still, to
be so fine, the way you work must be rather complex.
Could you tell us about the different steps you have
to take when printing any type of image?

L Complex I am but I am based on a rather simple
principle, the immiscibility of oil and water. My
masters draw on my body with a fat hydrophobic
medium, and surprisingly enough you can create
very fragile illustrations with an oily medium
of that type. Then I am covered with a chemical
solution that penetrates my pores, framing the
image with a hydrophilic layer that will not allow
the printing ink to get into in the blank areas.
I am then sent to the press on which I am covered,
thanks to a roll, with a special ink that only gets
to the hydrophobic areas, to the original drawing.
Later on, I meet the paper under the press, and
the image is born...

JP Thank you for clarifying all this. But I still have thing
I'd like to understand. On another matter, do you
feel endangered by the post digital printing tech-

niques now that your off-set grand-son is around?

L   As is the case with any analog printing technique,
    yes, I suppose I am somehow in a «weak» position.
    This much said, I believe that the fact that I am
    a slow, complex and rather hard process makes me
    gain value compared to other fast processes.
    I believe that the relationship one can have to
    a print that can take as much as 12 hours of work
    is not the same as with something that can be
    printed by pressing the print button on a computer
    screen. I believe that I will still be used by masters
    who will want to experience the printing process
    rather than just use it as a tool of reproduction.

JP I hope so too, it would be a shame to forget about
    the artistic qualities of print, in general. Thank you
    very much; Mr Litho for those clarifications and
    wise words.

Christopher Breu
THE INSISTENCE OF THE MATERIAL: THEORIZING MATERIALITY AND BIOPOLITICS IN THE ERA OF GLOBALIZATION

We are summoning a new materialism in response to a sense that the radicalism of the dominant discourses which have flourished under the cultural turn is now more or less exhausted. We share the feeling current among many researchers that the dominant constructivist orientation to social analysis is inadequate for the contemporary context of biopolitics and global political economy.

Diana Coole and Samantha Frost (2010)

Thinking Materiality: A Necessary Contradiction
This essay takes materiality as its object. In doing so, it is, by necessity, inadequate to this object.1 I begin from the premise that various forms of materiality

in contemporary social existence—the materiality of the body, the object world of late-capitalist life, the material elements of political-economic production, the various forms of materiality we group under the signifier "nature"—cannot be adequately or completely accounted for by language. I take this contradiction as my fundamental preoccupation. My argument attempts to attend to what Diana Coole and Samantha Frost describe as the "restlessness and intransigence of materiality" and what Richard Terdiman posits as "the brute and often brutal difficulty of materiality," even as it recognizes the inability of language, representation, or theory to fully do so (Coole and Frost 2010, 1; Terdiman 2005, 14).

However, I do not take the inability of language to fully account to its object as a reason to turn away from the attempt at such an account. Instead, in an era in which economic and cultural production have become increasingly fascinated with the virtual, the immaterial, and the textual, I think it becomes crucial to theorize the material. It also is crucial to theorize the material in an age in which political and economic organization have taken on a decidedly biopolitical and thanatopolitical character.

To broadly summarize, for the moment, what are actually very distinct deployments of these concepts by a range of theorists, biopolitics and its deathly double, thanatopolitics, describe the direct management of life and death by political and economic power.[2]

ESSAY #2

My characterization of this era as simultaneously one preoccupied with immateriality and an one defined by biopolitics is not coincidental. Both the privileging of the so-called immaterial or virtual and the idea of complete biopolitical control imagine a material world that is a passive site of inscription and unproblematic manipulation. Undergirding both notions is a social logic that imagines signification to be coterminous with existence—that the way in which we represent or narrate the world is adequate to the world that is. My theorization of materiality, thus, tries to posit it as a limit and an outside to biopolitics, even as it also charts the way in which material life is shaped in ever more intimate ways by biopolitics, thanatopolitics, and biopolitical production. Materiality, in this formulation, can be likened to biopolitics' and virtuality's unconscious flipside, one that resists integration with the world of symbolic representation. For reasons bound up with the very dynamic I am describing, then, it is crucial to both theorize the material and keep in mind the way in which such theorizations are always inadequate to their objects. My project is thus organized around two imperatives: (i) theorize and attend to the material in the era of biopolitics and (ii) recognize language's limits in doing so.

As the epigraph from Coole and Frost indicates, I am not alone in wishing to tarry with the material. There has been widespread frustration at the limits of the cultural/linguistic turns in much recent theore-

115

CHRISTOPHER BREU

tical writing. As Stacy Alaimo puts it: "What has been notably excluded by the 'primacy of the cultural' and the turn toward the linguistic and the discursive is the 'stuff' of matter" (2008, 242). In contrast, to the linguistic and cultural turns, Alaimo and Susan Hekman propose what they term the "material turn" in their ground-breaking collection, *Material Feminisms* (2008, 6). I too want to theorize the stuff of matter and thus ally myself with what Alaimo and Hekman call the material turn and what Frost and Coole (2010) term the "new materialisms." In doing so, however, I also want to indicate that it is important to retain certain concepts from the cultural and linguistic turns, specifically subjectivity, language, and culture, even as we transform these concepts in order to make them more materialist. It seems important that we retain aspects of the cultural and linguistic turns precisely to mark the differences and antagonisms between the cultural and the material even as we also chart their interlardings and interweavings. One of the dangers of a wholesale rejection of the cultural turn is that we merely invert its logic, rewriting the same set of theoretical moves that characterized the cultural turn onto the material. If we really want to be attentive to the challenge that the heterogeneity of materiality presents to cultural and critical theory, we need to think about how various forms of materiality differ from, intermix with, and place limits on the cultural and linguistic, rather than just merely supersede or replace them.

ESSAY #2

I also want to echo Sara Ahmed (2010) and Sonia Kruks (2010) in suggesting that the new theoretical work of the material turn needs to be brought into dialogue with older forms of materialist scholarship. Thus, while I will draw upon much of the new materialist work in areas as diverse as biopolitics, feminist theory, critical science studies, thing studies, object studies, and political-ecology, I will put it in dialogue with the rich materialist traditions associated with Marxism and psychoanalytic theory in order to theorize the relationship of materiality to subjectivity and subjective embodiment on the one hand and political-economy and globalization on the other.

In what follows, then, I will first provide a brief account of the value and limits of the cultural turn. I will then map out some of the trajectories of the recent material turn, putting it in dialogue with older materialist approaches and suggesting the ways in which we can draw on both older and newer approaches to the question of materiality in order to theorize the bodies, objects, biopolitics, political ecology, and political economy in our globalizing present.

Beyond the Cultural and Linguistic Turns

Culture and language: these are the totemic words around which literary and cultural studies have circled for much of the last thirty years. Even as the critique of the linguistic and cultural turns has become more forceful in recent years, it is still not uncommon in

CHRISTOPHER BREU

contemporary scholarship and pedagogy to find each of these terms elevated to the position of a placeholder for social life itself.[3] Indeed, in the moment of their greatest ascendency, the 1980s and 1990s, it was common to hear each of these concepts evoked in ways that refused the ability to posit their limits or theorize that which resided outside of or in tension with them. Instead, each term became part of a self-contained "language-game" (to use the Wittgenstein-derived rhetoric of the time) that allowed, for all the attention to otherness, no space for the radically heterodox to be understood, or even posited.

This is far from what was intended by these epistemological "turns" and by the forms of social constructivism associated with them. Indeed, each of these turns emerged around the same time for reasons both political and epistemological. They emerged as a way of challenging ideological habits of thought associated with earlier moments of cultural or political *doxa*.

The power of the constructivist interventions is nowhere more palpable than in the theoretical impetus they have provided in the last thirty years for the theoretical critiques of racism, sexism, homophobia, and class habitus.[4] Many of these interventions have turned around the critique of the ideological production of cultural difference as natural difference and the ways in which a reified or essentialized conception of nature was used to justify various forms of social inequality. This critique of various processes of "naturalization" remains an invaluable and very necessary contribution made by social construction to theoretical critique. And indeed, social construction continues to remind us, as do theorists of discursive productivity such as Foucault and Judith Butler, that we should posit that which is outside of culture and language with the utmost care, lest we reproduce the forms of essentialism that the critique of the process of naturalization was designed to undo.

The Material Turn

One of the ways to know that a concept has become part of a problematic orthodoxy is when it can no longer theorize its limits. This is precisely what has happened to the terms, culture and language as they are typically invoked and metaphorized in literary and cultural studies. However, more recently, interdisciplinary work in the humanities, the social sciences, and critical science studies has pushed against this orthodoxy, attending to that which cannot be understood as fully cultural or discursively constituted.

The recent material turn in scholarship holds a great deal of promise. As a corrective to the cultural and linguistic turns that preceded it, the recent turn to theorizing and tarrying with various forms of materiality has been salutary, working to demonstrate the limits of both textual- and social-constructivism as dominant paradigms for work in the humanities. This materialist turn has taken many forms, from the object worlds

CHRISTOPHER BREU

traced by Bill Brown (2004) and Ian Bogost (2012), through the engagement with the agency of things in the ecotheoretical work of Bruno Latour (2004b) and Jane Bennett (2010), the emphasis on biological life in much recent work in biopolitics, feminist theory, and animal studies, to the emphasis on geopolitics and political economy in globalization theory and Marxist accounts of neoliberalism.

The Material and Biological Body

It is in the context of the cultural and linguistic turns that preceded it that the materialist turn has made its important interventions. Thus social-constructivist accounts of the body have been complicated by the emphasis on the biological and material body in the writings of Rosi Braidotti (2002), Elizabeth Grosz (1994), and Anne Fausto-Sterling (2000) and in the work collected in *Material Feminisms* (Alaimo and Hekman 2008). Elizabeth Grosz initiates this line of inquiry, with her watershed text, *Volatile Bodies*, with its emphasis on producing a theory that can account for "some sort of articulation, or even disarticulation, between the biological and the psychological" (1994, 23). Working in a similar vein as Grosz, Braidotti (2002) has produced a vitalist theory of feminist embodiment, one that draws on the work of Luce Irigaray (1993) and Gilles Deleuze and Félix Guattari (1987), in order to emphasize the intertwining of the biological and the subjective as they are bound up in a process of becoming. Perhaps most compellingly for the work I am undertaking, Anne Fausto-Sterling (2000) presents an account of intersex that demonstrates the way in which the material and biological body of the intersex individual disrupts and challenges the sexed meanings projected and often violently inscribed on this body by the medical establishment. The essays collected in *Material Feminisms* work in different ways to theorize the materiality of the body and of biological processes, often in relationship to other forms of materiality, including the material dimensions of ecosystems.

All of these theorists push our understanding of embodiment beyond the parameters of either cultural or discursive construction. Indeed, each of them asks us to reckon with the materiality of a body that resists as well as conforms to cultural scripts. Moreover, what is particularly notable about the work of Fausto-Sterling and other theorists of intersex and trans-sex such as Alice Dreger (2000) and C. Jacob Hale (1998; 2008) is that they produce an account of the materiality of the biological body that does not reproduce the binary of sex. Thus, their work maintains the necessary critique of sexual binarism that is central to Butler's work, while also insisting on the materiality of the body as that which can and often does resist or exceed discursive construction. My own, psychoanalytic account of the body is deeply indebted to the materialist line of inquiry opened up by Grosz, Braidotti, Fausto-Sterling and the essayists in *Material Feminisms*.

CHRISTOPHER BREU

Many of these theorists emphasize the way in which the opposition between language and the material body can be deconstructed or seen as part of a material continuum. Such an emphasis is important, demonstrating the ways in which the linguistic and the material, subjects and objects interpenetrate. What Grosz describes, drawing on Lacan's category of the imaginary and reworking Freud's notion of the body ego, as an "imaginary anatomy," represents one particularly fruitful account of such an intermixing. As she articulates it, this imaginary anatomy is an also necessary locus where the biological and the subjective intersect (1994, 37). It is in the imaginary where the biological body becomes encoded with subjective meanings, even as it is crucial to recognize the often radical discontinuity between the body ego as a map of the body and the material body itself. The body ego's image of the body is shaped and refigured by desire and by the erotogenic mapping of the body—thus certain organs and surfaces are emphasized, while others are deemphasized, if not altogether occluded.

This disjunction between the imaginary and the material body suggests the importance of not just theorizing their overlap or interpenetration but also theorizing the ways in which signification and the more obdurate materialities of the body are importantly distinct and sometimes form in opposition to each other. While much of the materialist work on embodiment emphasizes the way in which the opposition between language and the material body can be undone, I want to lay stress in the other direction: that in order for us to fully attend to the materiality of our bodies, we need to insist on the ways in which the materiality of language and the materiality of the body not only interpenetrate and merge (particularly in the construction of our imaginary bodies), but are also importantly distinct and sometimes form in opposition to each other.

In order to theorize the material body that is in tension with, even as it is also bound up with, the imaginary body, I deploy a version of Lacan's (1988, 97-98; 1992, 43-70; 1993, 190-1) concept of the real. In contradistinction to the imaginary and symbolic, the real is one of the most elusive and controversial concepts in Lacan as well as one of the categories that underwent the most revision during the course of his teaching. It is elusive in part because that it is nature. It is easier to define it negatively, in terms of what it is not rather than in terms of what it is: the real is everything that remains outside of the symbolic and the imaginary, even as it haunts and disrupts the logics of both. Thus the real can be used to talk about trauma, death, the fetishistic status of what Lacan calls the *objet petit* a (or little bit of the other), and about uncoded materiality itself. While Slavoj Žižek, in his more recent writings, has emphasized the real's nonmaterial nature, as a gap, hole, or excess around which the symbolic is organized (2006, 26), I want to emphasize a materialist understanding of the term. This latter understanding of the real comes out of developmentalist accounts of Lacan. Thus the child begins, as a "fragmented body," in the locus of the real, a realm of uncoded materiality in which the line between inside and outside, self and other is not yet formed (Lacan 2006, 78). Bruce Fink helpfully entitles this first version of the real as uncoded materiality Real1 or R1, and contrasts it with the functioning of the real with the advent of the symbolic (what he terms Real2 or R2) (1995, 26-8), in which its status becomes closer to what Žižek (2006, 26) describes as the gap or what Lacan describes as the *objet* a, or the little piece of the real—of the body of the other or an object—that functions as a fetish. Yet there is always a relationship between R2 and R1—the various avatars of R2, such as the *objet* a, but also trauma, and the gap in the symbolic, point to those forms of materiality that have not been fully coded by the symbolic and thus recall the undifferentiated state that preceded symbolization.

I use this notion of the real as uncoded materiality in order to talk about the aspects of the body that exceed or refuse our symbolic and imaginary constructions of it. In theorizing this real body (which should be understood as distinct from any naïve empirical understanding of the "reality" of the body—the real is always a relational term), it enables me to articulate the resistance that the body has, for example to gendered, sexual, and cultural scripts as well as to contemporary scientific, philosophical, and theoretical accounts and mappings of the body. My use of this concept of the real body, then allows me to attend to what Anne Fausto-Sterling has theorized as the resistance of bodies—particularly intersex bodies—to the sexual scripts placed on them by culture, by the medical establishment, and even sometimes by the subject herself (2000, 60-3). In emphasizing this real body, I am not trying to maintain a Cartesian mind/body split. Our thinking selves and our speaking selves are always embodied and this embodiment shapes the knowledge and speech we produce. Yet, I think it is dangerous (and still a legacy of the linguistic turn) to imagine that all forms of materiality are continuous with language and can be understood in terms of linguistic models.

Objects, Things, and Political-Ecology
Another strain of recent materialist work can be grouped under the banner of object studies or thing studies. This work encompasses both the material culture studies championed by Bill Brown in his accounts of the centrality of material objects in American culture (2004), the queer phenomenological work of Sara Ahmed (2006), the alien phenomenology of Ian Bogost (2012), and the eco-theoretical work of Bruno Latour (2004b; 2007, 63-86) and Jane Bennett (2010) on the agency enacted by matter and material objects. Each of these theorists has disrupted the cultural turn's central preoccupation with subjectivity by pointing out the material objects and entities that are obscured by this focus. If the cultural and linguistic turns decentered the subject, it was

CHRISTOPHER BREU

still the subject who was the focus of this decentering. Ahmed, Bogost, Brown, Bennett and Latour have each, in different ways, pushed us to attend to the objects and forms of matter that lie outside of this exclusive focus on subjectivity. These material things are central to culture yet irreducible to it. Both Latour and Bennett, moreover, have demonstrated the ways in which objects and materiality are not merely recalcitrant, but exert a force—what Bennett terms "agency" and what Latour calls "speech"—in relationship to culture and its constructions (Bennett 2010, 1 & 21; Latour 2004b, 67). As Latour and Bennett's use of terminology such as voice and agency to describe this force suggests, their construction of the material world is still filtered, to a greater extent than I think they realize, through the paradigms of the cultural and linguistic turns.

Yet their visions are powerful ones and help us to imagine a social and ecological world outside of the cultural and linguistic conceived either as absolute limits or the total sum of what is. I draw on their insights in order to theorize the material and the work it does as an actant (to use the term that Latour and Bogost derive from literary theory and which I like, in spite of its linguistic resonances, because of its emphasis on action). I will also employ Latour and Bennett's powerful conception of "political-ecology" as a way of talking about the political and economic stakes between the human and the nonhuman and as a way of conceptualizing what Latour describes as "the collective" (which he defines as a "procedure for collecting associations of humans and nonhumans") (Latour 2004b, 238 & 246; Bennett 2010, 94). In contrast to Latour, however, I will use political ecology alongside of the more established term, political economy, because I think it is essential to maintain the economic critique advanced by Marxist and neomarxist theories and because this critique much too quickly falls out of the work of both Bennett and Latour.

If Bennett willfully errors on the side of anthropomorphism in her argument, I want to error towards the opposite, towards the radically nonhuman dimensions of the material, including, at points, the materialities and material prostheses of our own bodies. I am thus more interested in theorizing the resistance and recalcitrance of the object, as well as to its heterogeneity to (as well as intersections with) human motivation and action. In emphasizing the recalcitrance and heterogeneity of objects, I draw on Bogost's reworking of Graham Harman's and Levi Bryant's object-oriented ontology to "embrace the multifarious complexity of being among all things" as it "exceeds our own grasp of the being of the world" (Bogost 2012, 5, 30). Yet, since I am still interested in theorizing the relationship between subject and object, even as I want to place more emphasis on the object side of the pole, I also draw on Sara Ahmed's queer phenomenology, which emphasizes the way in which subjects are "oriented" to specific objects (2006, 58). One alternative or "queer" orientation would be to recognize and respect, rather than try to master, the heterogeneity of the object or objects (Ibid., 161). Such an orientation would begin to give the material its due, to attend to what Theodor Adorno describes as the "object's preponderance" (1973, 183).

While writing in an earlier moment of materialist critique, Adorno presents an account of the negative relationship between subject and object that can be quite valuable for the work undertaken by the (current) material turn. For Adorno, the pressing question of the moment in which he was writing, a moment defined by what he described as the administered society and which can also be understood as a Keynesian version of biopolitics, is that of the status of the object. For Adorno, as he and Max Horkheimer articulate it in the co-authored *Dialectic of Enlightenment*, the heterogeneity of the object was threatened by instrumental rationality and the logics of identity and equivalence that it underwrites. The qualitative dimensions of objects were effaced in a political economic and scientific logic in which "equivalence itself has become a fetish" (1999, 17). Adorno also saw this same logic at work in language, especially as it was being reshaped by the dictates of instrumental rationality. For him, it was "the concept" itself, as it was used by the subject to appropriate the object, that inevitably did a form of epistemological violence to this self-same object: "The prevailing trend in epistemological reflection was to reduce objectivity more and more to the subject. This very tendency needs to be reversed" (1973, 176). His positing of what he termed negative dialectics becomes his way of reversing this tendency. Negative dialectics insist on the object's preponderance by refusing to posit its full negation via the subject in the movement of the dialectic. This is a radicalization of the Hegelian or Marxian dialectic, in the sense that it theorizes an aspect of the object that is not transformed or sublated in the movement of the dialectic, but remains resistant to the dialectic's movement.

Such a negative dialectics, then, allows us to attend to subject's orientations (in Ahmad's terms) toward the object and the way in which objects are transformed via their encounter with subjects, while still emphasizing the irreducibility and heterogeneity of objects (their alien qualities in Bogost's terms) to human fantasies of mastery. Such a negative dialectics also suggests the theoretical limitations of many accounts of biopolitics in not theorizing the resistance and intransigence of objects, and of subjects for that matter, to the direct political and economic management of life. It is the engagement with biopolitics as part of the recent material turn that I will address next.

Biopolitics and Thanatopolitics
The recent theoretical engagement with biopower and biopolitics, as well as its ghastly inversion, thanatopolitics, holds much promise for the material turn.

CHRISTOPHER BREU

Both biopolitics and thanatopolitics present versions of politics in which biological life itself and its cessation in death are directly invested and managed by political and economic forms of power. Thus it is an understanding of power that attends directly to the shaping and management of biological life. As such, its relevance to the material turn should be obvious. It also, as Adele Clarke et al., Giorgio Agamben, Roberto Esposito, and Michael Hardt and Antonio Negri differently articulate it, a growing form of power in the neoliberal and globalizing present. Yet as powerful as biopolitics and thanatopolitics are as concepts, I think they need to be theorized more fully in relationship to both materiality and political economy. Before doing so, however, I will provide a brief overview of the different theories of biopolitics and how they theorize the relationship between power and biological life.

As Michel Foucault posits in *The History of Sexuality Volume One* (1978, 135-59) and in three different volumes of his recently published lectures at the Collège de France, biopolitics is a form of power that takes life itself as its focus, particularly as it is regulated and ordered by the workings of governmentality in terms of technologies of population, statistics, public health, and eugenics. While Foucault's accounts of biopolitics in *The History of Sexuality V.1* and "*Society Must Be Defended*" (2003) are his most commonly cited and have exerted the most influence on scholars such as Agamben, Mbembe, and Esposito, his account in *The*

Birth of Biopolitics (2010) presents a crucial development of his thesis, one that ties it directly to economics and specifically to the growth of neoliberalism in the second half of the twentieth century (and which continues apace into the twenty-first century).[5]

While Foucault never fully theorizes the connection, he suggests that the relationship between biopolitics and neoliberalism can be adduced in connection to the neoliberal concept of "human capital" as the means by which human life and biology are regulated under neoliberalism (2010, 226-9). Human capital assumes that all aspects of human existence can be quantified and thus regulated by the market. Thus, all aspects of what formerly were understood to be civil society and the public trust (such as healthcare, education, childcare, social wellbeing, etc.) under Keynesianism should be privatized in order to maximize the production of human capital. Moreover, the maximization of human capital is the responsibility of individuals; it should be a competitive system, so that there is an impetus to maximize one's share of capital.

The effects of this form of privatization are manifold and have a direct impact on embodiment and the construction of materiality. The body is shaped and reshaped via the demands of human capital, from the violence done to the working body in an economy that no longer protects workers to the uneven forms of what Adele Clarke et al. have termed biomedicalization (2010, 1-87). Under the regime of biomedicalization, medicine is defined as a process of the maximization and normitivization of health, while it is further privatized and individuals are increasingly interpellated by a moral discourse of wellness (in which the maintenance of our health becomes entirely our own responsibility). What is crucial to grasp, though, for other accounts of the biopolitical is that what were once defined as the rights of citizens and thus were tied to notions of national and democratic sovereignty are now defined products of the market or of governmentality. Circumventing earlier, if radically imperfect, forms of mediation via notions of citizenship and sovereignty, biopolitics directly shapes and invests life itself.

Drawing on Giorgio Agamben (1998) and Foucault's accounts (2003), Achille Mbembe has theorized the application of biopolitics to the context of colonialism and neocolonialism, arguing compellingly that colonialism exerts direct control over human life, "dictating who may live and who must die" (2003, 11). Thus, Mbembe crucially adds the element of negativity to what Foucault (1978) theorizes in terms of positive power. Roberto Esposito develops this notion of the politics of death even further with his conception of thanatopolitics. Esposito turns to the context of the Holocaust to theorize the way in which biopolitics turns into its deathly opposite, thanatopolitics. He argues that this transformation from a positive (if still violent) form of governmentality into its negative double takes place around the logic of immunity. For him, biopolitics is always split or double—privileging one community, or nation, or group as immune while marking another segment of the population as outside the *cordon sanitaire*. Esposito argues that in the name of immunity biopolitics turns around into thanatopolitics, justifying violence against those who are outside the sphere of protection. Thus in the name of maximizing the health and vitality of all of those who are immunized in the body politic, biopolitics becomes a ceaseless campaign of death (since health itself can never be guaranteed) (Esposito 2008, 44-77).

Esposito's and Mbembe's different accounts of thanatopolitics add a crucial dimension of negativity to theorizing the effects of contemporary biopolitics. They also push beyond the limits of social constructivism by theorizing death, something that was never really fully possible within the sphere of the cultural and linguistic turns (one could theorize the representations of death or discourses around death, but not the material finality of death itself for organic beings). It is no accident that death, for Lacan (1977, 79-90), is one of the dimensions of the real; it is a phenomenon that as a material process refuses full representation in the space of the symbolic.

While neither Esposito nor Mbembe really theorize this, I want to suggest that thanatopolitics can be theorized in political-economic terms as well: the way in which maximizing profit or human capital on one scene or in one locus around the globe often produces

CHRISTOPHER BREU

death (in the form of starvation, reduced life expectancy, economic neglect) on another. Michael Hardt and Antonio Negri are the theorists who articulate most fully an economic understanding of biopolitics. They articulate what they term "biopolitical production" as the core component of economic production in the neoliberal present (2000, 30). Hardt and Negri's elaboration of the political economic to the category of biopolitics is both necessary and extremely valuable. Indeed, given the centrality of economic power in our globalizing present, the exclusive emphasis on governmentality in most accounts of biopolitics feels, at best, inadequate. For this reason, Hardt and Negri's economic reconceptualization of the term is both timely and necessary for thinking about life in a world in which, as Adele Clarke et al. demonstrate, the economic and the bodily are becoming ever more complexly and intimately intertwined (2010, 1-44).

Yet even as Hardt and Negri link biopolitics to economics with their conception of biopolitical production they do so in the name of what they term "immaterial production" or the forms of financial, service, and affective labour that represent the leading sectors of the global economy (2004, 114-115). While they are right to emphasize the importance of these sites of production, their conceptualization of such form of production as "immaterial" becomes easily complicit with the fantasies of dematerialization that form one of the central ideologies of our digitalizing present.

ESSAY #2

Hardt and Negri are careful to argue that immaterial production is intimately tied to material production. Yet they stake their whole revolutionary vision on the forms of autonomous productivity that are central to the relatively high-end and high-pay work associated with immaterial production. Thus the material is finally backgrounded by their account, not just the recalcitrant materiality of bodies, which they theorize like Foucault, Agamben, Mbembe, and Esposito, as passive sites upon which biopolitical and thanatopolitical forms of power inscribe themselves, but also many of the recalcitrantly material processes of late capitalist production itself.

In order for biopolitics, thanatopolitics, and biopolitical production to realize their full critical potential as analytic categories, then, I want to suggest that they need to be rethought in relationship to the insistent and resistant materiality of bodies and of large sectors of the production process itself. This is not to situate the body or materiality as fully outside the sphere of culture. Indeed, as much biopolitical thought has demonstrated, the history of the last half century can be productively thought of in terms of the increasing ability of culture to shape and discipline the body and for it to socialize and commodify ever more fully different aspects of everyday life. Rather, it is to refuse to make the material and the cultural coincident. For even as the cultural and the discursive shape our bodies in ever more intimate and subtle ways, the

CHRISTOPHER BREU

materiality of our bodies resists and interacts with such dynamics in ways neither fully controllable nor predictable. Moreover, the bodily and the biological, even as they are transformed by biopolitical and economic processes, also form sites of limit and resistance to those very same processes (limits and resistances that are historically specific and changing but partially determining nonetheless). Such an emphasis resists the fantasies of bodily transcendence that are increasingly central, as N. Katherine Hayles (1999, 1-25; 2010, 23-41) has so cogently pointed out, to our digital age, particularly in a psycho-geographical space of the global North which is fully immersed in the transformations produced by "immaterial production." In an era in which the dominant ideology of digitalization is the virtual imagined as a process of dematerialization, it becomes especially important for reasons both political-economic and ecological to attend to the material resources and still very material forms of production that underpin these fantasies of virtuality.

Political Economy and Globalization
The emergence of globalization theory and the resurgence of work in political economy can also be considered part of the material turn. While globalization theory has both cultural and a political-economic components (not to mention ecological, political, and environmental components), in almost all its guises it has placed an emphasis on the limits of the cultural by emphasizing it

as only one dynamic in the process of globalization. This break with the limits of the cultural turn is evident in the work done in globalization theory by Arif Dirlik and David Harvey, with their different meditations (Dirlik 2001; Harvey 2005; 2010) on the relationship between neoliberalism, post-Fordism and the ideology of the cultural turn, and by the large-scale political-economic interpretations of the capitalist world system in the work of world-systems theorists such as Aníbal Quijano (2008), Immanuel Wallerstein (2000; Wallerstein and Quijano 1992) and Giovanni Arrighi (2010). It is also evident in the impressively integrative work of Saskia Sassen on global cities (1999; 2001), which attends to the political-economic without giving the sphere of culture a short shrift.

I use world-systems theory and Sassen's and Harvey's social-geographical understandings of globalization in order to provide a longer and more complex account of the spatial and temporal dynamics of globalization than is usually present in contemporary-oriented accounts of the phenomenon. While the dynamics of globalization have accelerated greatly in the last thirty years (what has been termed "the era of globalization"), the process as both Paul Jay (2010, 33-53) and the world-systems theorists argue, needs to be understood as part of a much longer dynamic, one that has its roots in what Immanuel Wallerstein terms "the 'long' sixteenth century" and which takes the history of European imperialism, which in this account is bound up with the history of capitalism, as part of its purview (2000, 93). As Ian Baucom (2005, 27-8) has also noticed, this long-view of globalization enables us to theorize the dynamics of capitalist development in a more spatially and temporally complex and recursive way. Thus, as Aníbal Quijano (2008) argues, so-called primitive accumulation (or what Harvey nicely renames "accumulation by dispossession"), in which resources and land are appropriated wholesale by the capitalist (and often the colonialist) class does not just occur at the beginning of capitalism but instead represents a recurring dynamic within all phases of capitalism. This understanding of accumulation by dispossession enables us to attend to the appropriation of the material (of the minerals and resources of the earth, of the land, of bodies themselves as they are defined as possessions) that subtend the exploitation of wage labour and the production of commodities within capitalist production. For Quijano, even wage labour itself is the exception rather than the rule in Latin America (and I would add Africa)—one that is tied to whiteness. While the industrial proletariat as well as the new service proletariat are exploited via wage labour, this labour is often dependent upon unwaged labour (or directly biopolitical and often than a topolitical) labour on another scene. Thus, the dynamics of accumulation by dispossession, and the forms of imperialism to which they are bound, form what Slavoj Žižek terms the obscene underside to the dynamics of capitalist wage labour (1994, 57).

ESSAY #2

While there is certainly nothing new about political economy, with its genesis, according to the canonical narrative, in the eighteenth-century writings of Adam Smith, there has been a notable rehabilitation of it as a discipline in the last ten to fifteen years. During the peak of the cultural and linguistic turns, political economy appeared to be woefully out of step, a moribund discipline with an attenuated notion of culture as a mere reflection of an economic infrastructure. However the last ten to fifteen years or so have seen a veritable resurgence of political economy as a tool for social analysis. Even fields in which the critique of political economy was sharpest, such as cultural studies and queer theory, have recently produced work in a political-economic vein. Thus writers like Robert Babe (2010) in cultural studies and Rosemary Hennessy (2000) and Kevin Floyd (2009) in queer theory have produced rich theorizations of the intersection of the political-economic and the cultural.

While political economy is often considered a materialism of the Marxist kind rather than the materialism of physical matter that I have generally been addressing, there is a relationship between the two forms of materialism, one that is sometimes obscured in the present by the emergence of various forms of immaterial production and by what David Harvey describes as financialization. Marx's notion of materialism is organized around the ability of humans to effectively use and control the forms of physical matter associated with the earth and its products. He links this notion of the physical transformation of the earth to the various modes of production and the development of the productive forces and the means of production each one enables. Where this gets complicated is when the products of the capitalist mode of production become increasingly dematerialized as in the affective, service, electronic and financial sectors. In the context of these newer political-economic developments, it becomes necessary to trace the material underpinnings and material forms of production upon which they rest.

One way of attending to the material underpinnings of ostensibly immaterial production is suggested by Immanuel Wallerstein in his book, *The Decline of American Power*. In it he presents Fordism and post-Fordism, usually periodized as radically distinct periods, as A and B phases of a single economic cycle, what he terms a Kondratieff cycle. In such a cycle material production is central to the A phase and financial accumulation is central to the B phase, yet the two phases have to be understood in relationship to each other and as dominant tendencies in what is an interconnected and interlarded process (2003, 49-52). Thus, elements that are subordinate, yet present, in the A phase become dominant in the B phase and vice versa. This allows for an understanding of the way in which post-Fordism and the forms of immaterial production usually associated with it are absolutely dependent upon the forms of material production and the built environment produced by Fordism and by forms of industrial and material production that continue into post-Fordism. This theorization, then, allows me to trace the material underpinnings and structures beneath the flickering images and seemingly insubstantial commodities of the era of immaterial production.

Conclusion: A Politics of Materiality

We need to attend to such material structures and economic processes as they intersect with our material bodies and the material parameters of our ecosystems. To my mind we have just begun to tarry with the material. It is my supposition that in such a tarrying we can begin to produce a thought more readily equipped to deal with the political, economic, ecological, and, yes, cultural challenges that face us in the twenty-first century. A more materialist conception of biopolitics and thanatopolitics, one that does not take matter as a passive site for inscription, appropriation, and manipulation but instead understands it as exerting resistance and action in its own right would enable us to more effectively theorize the intersections of the political, the economic and the material. It would also enable us to theorize the limits of biopolitics and thanatopolitics as forms of power.

A reconceptualized understanding of subjectivity, one that situates it more fully in relationship to the material and biological body, will similarly help us to theorize the limits of biopolitical forms of power (which tend to treat subjectivity itself as fully subsumed within the workings of power). It will allow us to retain what is best about the cultural turn—the attention to human action and self-reflexivity— while situating these dynamics within the material strictures and insistences of the body. A non-reductive conception of the biological and material limits of the body and of other aspects of existence will thus enable us to combat the idealism that has inflected too much of the work in the cultural and linguistic turns.

Similarly, an attention to the insistence and resistance of the material would insure that our models of political economy and political ecology do not become caught up in the fetishization of the immaterial or in the seemingly inverse, yet related, fantasy that we can fully predict, control, or manipulate the material. Such an account of the material would not only theorize its positive qualities, but also mark its negative refusals: the way in which aspects of materiality exceed our intellectual grasp and physical manipulations. It is in attending to the work of the negative that I find Lacan's account of the real, Adorno's account of the preponderance object, and Bogost's insistence on the object's partial autonomy being crucial.

But of course we need to not just mark the refusals of the material, but also begin to think of a new materialist politics. Such a politics will involve what Sara Ahmed posits as a different "orientation" towards the

ESSAY #2

material, one that is attentive to the experience of disorientation and queer or alternate orientations. Such a politics would also involve an ethics of what Stacy Alaimo (2008) describes as "transcorporality" in which we attend to the links and interconnections between our own corporeality and the corporeality and materialities of other beings and entities. Such a reconceptualized ethics would be part of a new understanding of the commons, one in which the actors are not only human but one in which all material beings and entities form a part. In such a conception of the commons, the material (including its negative resistances and refusals) would be central. It is for such a commons that we need to struggle in the neoliberal present.

Originally published in *Globalization Working Papers* 12/2 August 2012

1 I want to thank Robert O'Brien, Nancy Johnson, Rachel Zhou, Susie O'Brien, Tony Porter, Peter Walmsley, the two anonymous peer reviewers, and the rest of the Institute on Globalization and the Human Condition for their feedback on various drafts of this paper. The paper began as a presentation at the IGHC during my stay there in the fall of 2011. I also presented a version of the paper at Illinois State in the spring of 2012. Because of the wealth of generous feedback I received from both audiences, this is a much stronger paper than it would otherwise be. I also want to thank Nancy Johnson for doing a wonderful copy editing job on the final document. All remaining mistakes are my own. Finally, I want to thank the Institute for providing such a rich intellectual environment within which to pursue my research.

2 The texts I have in mind in thinking about biopolitics, biopolitical production, and thanatopolitics are: Foucault (1978; 2003; 2010), Agamben (1997), Hardt and Negri (2000; 2004; 2009), Mbembe (2003), Esposito (2008), and Clarke, Mamo, Fosket et al. (2010).

3 For some of the more compelling critiques of the linguistic, cultural, and rhetorical turns see: Hekman (2008), Hacking (1999), Latour (2004a), and Hennessy (2000).

CHRISTOPHER BREU

4   To name just a few examples, think how impoverished contemporary
    theories of gender and sexuality would be without the work of Judith
    Butler (1990), or contemporary work on race would be without the
    work of Omi and Winant (1994), or social class without the work of
    Pierre Bourdieu (1987).
5   My understanding of neoliberalism comes primarily from David Harvey
    (2005), Henry Giroux (2008), and Foucault (2010).

Works Cited

Adorno, Theodor W. 1973. *Negative dialectics*, trans. E.B. Ashton.
    London, UK: Continuum.
Adorno, Theodor W. and Max Horkheimer. 1999. *Dialectic of
    enlightenment*, trans. John Cumming. New York, NY: Continuum.
Agamben, Giorgio.1997. Homo sacer: sovereign power and bare life, trans.
    Daniel Heller-Roazen. Stanford, CA: Stanford University Press.
Ahmed, Sara. 2006. *Queer phenomenology: orientations, objects, others*.
    Durham, NC: Duke University Press.
—. 2010. Orientations matter, In *New materialisms: ontology, agency and
    politics*, ed. D. Coole and S. Frost, 234-57. Durham, NC: Duke University Press.
Alaimo, Stacy. 2008. Transcorporeal feminisms and the ethical space of
    nature. In *Material feminisms*, ed. S. Alaimo and S. Hekman, 237-64.
    Bloomington, IN: University of Indiana Press.
Alaimo, Stacy and Susan Hekman. 2008. Introduction: emerging models of
    materiality in feminist theory. In *Material feminisms*, ed. S. Alaimo
    and S. Hekman, 1-19. Bloomington, IN: University of Indiana Press.
Appadurai, Arun. 1997. *Modernity at large: cultural dimensions of
    globalization.* Minneapolis, MN: University of Minnesota Press.
Arrighi, Giovanni. 2010. *The long twentieth century: money, power, and the
    origins of our times, new and updated edition.* London, UK: Verso.
Babe, Robert. 2010. *Cultural studies and political economy: toward a
    new integration.* Lexington, KY: Lexington Books.
Baucom, Ian. 2005. *Specters of the Atlantic: finance capital, slavery,
    and the philosophy of history.* Durham, NC: Duke University Press.
Bennett, Jane. 2010. *Vibrant matter: a political ecology of things.*
    Durham, NC: Duke University Press.
Bogost, Ian. 2012. *Alien phenomenology, or what it's like to be a thing.*
    Minneapolis, MN: University of Minnesota Press.
Bourdieu, Pierre. 1987. *Distinction: a social critique of the judgment of
    taste*, trans. Richard Nice. Cambridge, MA: Harvard University Press.
Braidotti, Rosi. 2002. *Metamorphoses: towards a materialist theory of
    becoming.* London, UK: Polity Press.

Brown, Bill. 2004. *A sense of things: the object matter of American literature*. Chicago, IL: University of Chicago Press.

Butler, Judith. 1990. *Gender trouble: feminism and the subversion of identity*. New York, NY:Routledge.

—. 1993. *Bodies that matter: on the discursive limits of 'sex'*. New York, NY: Routledge.

Clarke, Adele, Laura Mamo, Jennifer Ruth Fosket, Jennifer R. Fishman, and Janet K. Shim eds. 2010. *Biomedicalization: technoscience, health, and illness in the U.S*. Durham, NC: Duke University Press.

Coole, Diana and Samantha Frost. 2010. Introducing the new materialisms. In *New materialisms*: ontology, agency, and politics, ed. D. Coole and S. Frost, 1-43. Durham, NC: Duke University Press.

Deleuze, Gilles and Félix Guattari. 1987. *A thousand plateaus: capitalism and schizophrenia*, trans. Brian Massumi. Minneapolis, MN: University of Minnesota Press.

Dirlik, Arif. 2001. *Global modernity: modernity in the age of capitalism*. London, UK: Paradigm Publishers.

Dreger, Alice. 2000. *Hermaphrodites and the medical invention of sex*. Cambridge, MA: Harvard University Press.

Esposito, Roberto. 2008. *Bíos: biopolitics and philosophy*, trans. Timothy Campbell. Minneapolis, MN: University of Minnesota Press.

Fausto-Sterling, Anne, 2000. *Sexing the body: gender politics and the construction of sexuality*. New York, NY: Basic Books.

Fink, Bruce. 1995. *The Lacanian subject: between language and jouissance*. Princeton, NJ: Princeton University Press.

Floyd, Kevin. 2009. *The reification of desire: toward a queer Marxism*. Minneapolis, MN: University of Minnesota Press.

Foucault, Michel.1978. *The history of sexuality. Volume one: an introduction*, trans. Robert Hurley. New York, NY: Vintage.

—. 2003. *"Society must be defended": lectures at the Collège de France 1975-1976*, trans. David Macey. New York, NY: Picador.

—. 2010. *The birth of biopolitics: lectures at the Collège de France, 1978-1979*, trans. Graham Burchell. New York, NY: Picador.

Freud, Sigmund. 1955. The interpretation of dreams. In The standard edition of the complete psychological works of Sigmund Freud, trans. James Strachey. London, UK: Hogarth Press.

Giroux, Henry. 2008. *Against the terror of neoliberalism: politics beyond the age of greed*. New York, NY: Paradigm Publishers.

Grosz, Elizabeth. 1994. *Volatile bodies: toward a corporeal feminism*. Bloomington, IN: Indiana University Press.

Hacking, Ian. 1999. *The social construction of what?* Cambridge, MA:

$Harvard University Press.

Hale, C. Jacob. 1998. Tracing a ghostly memory in my throat: reflections on ftm feminist voice and agency. In *Men doing feminism*, ed. Tom Digby, 99-130. New York, NY: Routledge.

—. 2008. Sex change, social change: reflections on identity, institutions, and imperialism. *Hypatia* 23 (1): 204-7.

Hardt, Michael and Antonio Negri. 2000. *Empire*. Cambridge, MA: Harvard University Press.

—. 2004. *Multitude: War and Democracy in the Age of Empire*. New York, NY: Penguin.

—. 2009. *Commonwealth*. Cambridge, MA: Harvard University Press.

Harvey, David. 2005. *A brief history of neoliberalism*. Oxford, UK: Oxford University Press.

—. 2010. *The enigma of capital and the crises of capitalism*. Oxford, UK: Oxford University Press.

Hayles, N. Katherine. 1999. *How we became post human: virtual bodies in cybernetics, literature, and informatics*. Chicago, IL: University of Chicago Press.

—. 2010. Traumas of code. In *Digital and other virtualities: renegotiating the image*, ed. A. Bryant and G. Pollock, 23-41. London, UK: I. B. Taurus.

Hekman, Susan. 2008. Constructing the ballast: an ontology for feminism. In *Material Feminisms*, ed.

S. Alaimo and S. Hekman, 85-119. Bloomington, IN: University of Indiana Press.

Hennessy, Rosemary. 2000. *Profit and pleasure: sexual identities in late capitalism*. New York: Routledge.

Irigaray, Luce. 1993. *An ethics of sexual difference*, trans. Carolyn Burke and Gillian C. Gill. Ithaca, NY: Cornell University Press.

Jay, Paul. 2010. *Global matters: the transnational turn in literary studies*. Ithaca, NY: Cornell University Press.

Kruks, Sonia. 2010. Simone de Beauvoir: engaging discrepant materialisms. In *New materialisms: ontology, agency, and politics* ed. D. Coole and S. Frost, 258-80. Durham, NC: Duke University Press.

Lacan, Jacques. 1977. *The four fundamental concepts of psychoanalysis: the seminar of Jacques Lacan book xi*, trans. Alan Sheridan. New York, NY: W. W. Norton and Company.

—. 1988. *The seminar of Jacques Lacan book ii: the ego in Freud's theory and in the technique of psychoanalysis, 1954-1955*, trans. Sylvana Tomaselli. New York, NY: W. W. Norton and Company.

—. 1992. *The ethics of psychoanalysis, 1959-1960: the seminar of*

Jacques Lacan book vii, trans. Dennis Porter. New York, NY: W. W. Norton and Company.

—. 1993. *The psychoses, 1955-1956: the seminar of Jacques Lacan book iii,* trans. Russell Grigg. New York, NY: W. W. Norton and Company.

—. 2006. *Écrits: the first complete edition in English,* trans. Bruce Fink. New York, NY: W. W. Norton and Company.

Latour, Bruno. 2004a. Why has critique run out of steam? From matters of fact to matters of concern. *Critical Inquiry* 30(2): 225-48.

—. 2004b. *The politics of nature: how to bring the sciences into social democracy.* Cambridge, MA: Harvard University Press.

—. 2007. *Reassembling the social: an introduction to actor-network-theory.* Oxford, UK: Oxford University Press.

Lévy, Pierre. 1998. *Becoming virtual: reality in the digital age.* New York, NY: Plenum.

Mbembe, Achille. 2003. Necropolitics (trans. Libby Meintjes). *Public Culture* 15(1): 11-40.

Omi, Michael and Howard Winant. 1994. *Racial formation in the United States: from the 1960s to the 1990s,* 2nd ed. New York, NY: Routledge.

Quijano, Aníbal. 2008. Coloniality of power, Eurocentrism, and Latin America. In *Coloniality at large: Latin America and the postcolonial debate,* eds. M. Moraña, E. Dussel, and C. A. Jáuregui, 181-224. Durham, NY: Duke University Press.

Saldívar, José David. 2012. *Trans-Americanity: subaltern modernities, global coloniality, and the cultures of Greater Mexico.* Durham, NC: Duke University Press.

Sassen, Saskia. 1999. *Globalization and its discontents: essays on the new mobility of people and money.* New York, NY: New Press.

—. 2001. *The global city: New York, London, Tokyo.* Princeton, NJ: Princeton University Press.

Terdiman, Richard. 2005. *Body and story: the ethics and practice of theoretical conflict.* Baltimore, MD: Johns Hopkins University Press.

Wallerstein, Immanuel. 2000. *The essential Wallerstein.* New York, NY: The New Press.

—. 2003. *The decline of American power.* New York, NY: The New Press.

Wallerstein, Immanuel and Aníbal Quijano. 1992. Americanity as a concept, or the Americas in the modern world system. *International Social Science Journal* 44: 549-557.

Žižek, Slavoj. 1994. *Metastases of enjoyment: six essays on woman and causality* London, UK: Verso.

—. 2006. *The parallax view.* Cambridge, MA: Massachusetts Institute of Technology Press.

Q & A WITH

MISS LETTERPRESS

Letter press is a peculiar character. Shy, yet proud. Our paths have crossed many times but we never had a real connection. Even though she has a clear connection to graphic design and her mechanism is quite accessible, just thinking of her summons a vision of long and complicated hours of work. But this interview revealed other things about her and it was a very interesting experience.

JP Hello Letter press, glad you could see me. To be honest to you and my readers, I have to say that I do not know you at all. Therefore, would you be so kind as to introduce yourself as if we were strangers ?

LP Good afternoon, there is no shame in not knowing me at all! Unlike a lot of printing techniques, the fact that I am letter-based makes me somehow unreachable. So to begin with… I was born in the mid-fifteen century and I had one dad only (which was a really unconventional situation back then), Johannes Gutenberg. My success was instantaneous and widespread even though it raised fears about the communication of knowledge and the protection of writing. I became one of the main text-based printing techniques used for books and other graphic works. Unfortunately,

Q & A WITH

fame doesn't last forever and the creation of off-set printing sent me into the shadows. Especially when you take into account that I am slow, expensive and hard while offset is fast, cheaper and precise. Yet, I am still in use nowadays. Especially by font nerds and other nostalgic graphic designers in search of authenticity.

JP Very well... It's already much clearer. Now that we know more about your history and position, would you be so kind as to describe your work process?

LP My pleasure. The idea is simple, it is the making that is perilous. Let's say that it could be a form of analog In design. Basically, my masters work with blocks of letters that they place in boxes called «beds» or «chases». Once the layout and text are settled, which is the longest and hardest part of the process, the bed full of letters is inked and sent to the press. This is where the inks meets the paper and the printing takes place. What is specific about is that very part of the process. The fact that the paper is pressed against the letters and therefore creates curves... This is what makes me so tactile and sensitive. And this is what offset is missing. In my opinion, this is something you cannot see in nowadays digital prints.

JP I am glad you brought that up! Indeed I am very interested in what you think of your position in the era of digital print. Are you rather scared, confident, enthusiastic...? Well, to be honest, I got scared when offset printing came around. Now that I am used to the idea of being an old mainstream technique, I can cope with it. Somehow ageing also made me wiser. And I have faith in myself, especially since nostalgia has become such a trend. I am to graphic design what a vintage chair is to furniture design, authentic.

LP Very well put , I am myself part of those graphic people who look for for authenticity through analog printing... Thank you for your time, Letter press, I hope we meet again.

ON THE MAKER AND THE MATTER… An interview with Johanna Drucker

Drucker, who specialises in the production of and reflection on printed matter. She is a writer and book artist known for her work in experimental typography and has published and lectured widely on topics related to the history of the book, contemporary art, graphic design, and digital aesthetics. She is also the Breslauer Professor of Bibliographical Studies in the Information Studies Department at the University of California, Los Angeles.

FL: As a start, I was hoping you could describe a making process of some sort, so we can use that as an illustration and a reference for the things we're speaking off.

JD: Sure, why don't I talk about *Diagrammatic Writing*, since that is a project you are familiar with? That was a project I had in mind for years, and like many of my projects, it was fundamentally conceptual, by which I simply mean idea-based, but needed to become concrete. The challenge of taking the idea of a fully self-referential concept into a material

INTERVIEW WITH J. DRUCKER

instantiation is like hatching a non-existent egg. I mean, you just can't sit on it, you know, because nothing will happen, but once you begin, then the embroidery sustains the enterprise. I made notes, lists of terms and concepts, thought about every aspect of the page and book as a set of relations and tried to embody them in the design. The back and forth of designing formats and writing about them became the substance of that work. I wanted to direct attention to the graphicality of thought processes in language. We think in forms, whether we are aware of that or not, and then forms return to us as pressures on thinking—does this fit, where does this go, is this language that should be before or after that language. These are all statements of relations, and relations are scored graphically. As you know, I used the term "diagrammatic" as a way to signal that the relations are active and dynamic, that they work and do work through their graphicality. The term "graphic" simply references surface organisation but that could be motivated by traditional approaches to display, harmony, proportion, and other conventional design principles. I mean, all designs *work* but they don't all say that they are working. So, with *Diagrammatic Writing* I had to find a way to take every statement a. in language and b. make it perform what it said.

FL: You have been critically and enthusiastically involved with print and print making for decades. Do you feel

NOTE #5

we are at a turning point in processing matter, now that
we have started to process in immaterial ways; are we
entering one next level closer to magic?

JD: I always resist the term "immaterial" since
computational technologies and processing are all
embedded in and depend upon multiple levels of
material, more, rather than less, than print—pro-
cessors, servers, networks, silicon, input/output
devices—the whole "stack" and network of it all.
But the fact that we work in processes that we can't
see, hear, touch, or perceive –in what I call "blind
media"—is what is different. As a person trained
to use my hands—to draw, paint, set type, print—I
am still always wanting to reach through the screen
to do the work. I guess when the haptic interface
is perfected we will have the possibility of virtual
making by hand and an illusion of direct manipulation of information in a somatic/embodied way.
Digital technologies are not just production technologies, but meta-production ones—they can reme-
diate every prior and other means and medium. This
makes them powerful, in the same way that photography was a meta-medium, capable of remediating
drawing, printmaking, type as well as functioning in
its own capacity as an indexical record of light. The
human ability to bring form into being and render
it legible to others is indeed magic, mind-boggling,
incredible. Primary semiosis—the making of signs

from the immanence of the world—that is truly magical to me. The reorganisation of matter, the ability to upload and download the stuff of atoms organised into form, that will be very convenient for travel—all one's "stuff" put onto a little flash drive in a "dematerialise to disk" and "re-materialise" cycle (d2d and reMat). I can't wait. That will solve the overhead bin wars that are currently making air travel so unsocial and anxiety-producing.

FL: Now for something fundamental that I'm curious to hear your opinion on: can our senses internalise the world we touch upon and is the inner self able to make sense of it (or could it simply be that we humans are self-fulfilled by our own cravings)?

JD: Have you ever seen the Werner Herzog film, *The Land of Silence and Darkness*? It is a profound meditation on the relations between cognition and sensorium. Herzog gives you an understanding of the way a deaf/blind woman constructs her world and it makes you aware of all the constructed-ness and limits on our own perception. I've been very influenced in this by the radical constructivist literature and its connection to animal perception—the ideas of ecological vision in J.J. Gibson's work where he shows how clearly the relation between perception and action shapes the visual "world" of birds, for instance. We are so attached to our sense that the world we "see" is a representation of the world that "is" "out there" that we lose sight (pun intended) of the vast amount of that world we never see—the neutrinos racing through our bodies, electromagnetic fields in our spaces, omnipresent ultraviolet rays, and even something as familiar as heat—these never register in our vision but they are powerfully present. As to being self-fulfilled by our own cravings…. Please! Remember, I was raised a Calvinist and cannot speak publically about such things, even to myself.

FL: As a maker, do you feel you can contribute to the positioning of an actual reality of production or…what can we learn from the practice of making?

JD: I think *poiesis*, making, is the fundamental act of giving form to thought and that it is as essential to the social activity of human beings as it is to the cultural life and identity of individuals. As an obsessive writer/maker, I feel like making is the only way to counter loss, the basic melancholy of being, in which the preciousness and ephemerality of life is so constantly, poignantly present at all moments. Leaving a trace, even if it vanishes eventually, provides the illusion that you can hold onto something in the flux and change of life.

FL: Is there any justification for a claim on contingency of authorship due to a relative autonomy of the material? Or simply put: is there any credibility in artists saying they felt the hand of the material, or don't know the outcome until it's done – and why should we believe such motivations?

JD: I think the answer depends on how process-oriented your work is. Working in letterpress with cast metal type, you are aware of how strongly the principle of "quadrature" imposes itself on the layout of the text—nice and square, line after line. But we preserve that linearity in the on-screen production of writing where it need not be the case—the pixel tapestry can register any image of language. So I wouldn't want to make a universal claim for the force or agency of material, only for the potential of material properties as one part of making. I think it depends on whether you are working with the material, or just using it. Not everyone who puts a book together has entered into an exploratory relationship with the paper, the binding, the ink, or other material components, after all. Lots of things just get produced as if material did not matter at all!

FL: Any last thoughts to share?

JD: We have just had a magnificent thunderstorm, which is rare in Southern California, and I am going to go out and have a run in the fresh-washed air which smells of newly charged ions. The availability of the world to perception is the greatest pleasure of being, after all, and I am constantly struck by how many distractions and screens (literal and figurative) people put between themselves and that experience. I'm not being judgmental, just surprised. Flying over the continent to go to East Coast last week I saw a beautiful snow-covered peak as we climbed past the San Gabriel mountains. I turned to the woman in the seat next to me to gesture to her out the window and was immediately rebuffed—I don't want to see, she said, I am watching a movie (it was a really crappy movie) and reading. I can't imagine not wanting to look at the world, which is always infinitely interesting by contrast to the productions of a thought-entertainment industry, which rarely is entertaining at all. But, I'm a snob and I don't care for processed thought any more than processed food. Life is short. Why bother with consuming poor matter if, as we do, we have the incredible luxury of alternatives. Maybe that just sounds corny and trite, or elitist and privileged—but, I mean, she will never again have a chance to see that mountain that way on that day and she didn't even want to look.

Q & A WITH

MISTER XYLOGRAPHY

Xylography... He's one of a kind. We met in primary school, a long time ago, I must have been around eight years old. And Xylo felt so accessible to me, especially at such a young age. He was playful and surprising, everything a kid could wish for. Our paths crossed recently, fourteen years later, and he was still the unexpected joyful character I had met a long time ago.

JP Hey, Xylography, it's very good to see you again after all these years!. It looks as if you have not changed at all. But please, could you explain to my fellow readers how you happened to become who you are now?

X Hey! Super exited to see you again too, buddy. So... Yeah, I am originally from Europe, Eastern Europe to be exact. My parents were German craftsmen called the Formschneider. It is funny that you mentioned I have not changed, it is very true since my physical appearance really does not betray my age, especially when you know that I was actually born around the fifteenth century, and that my Chinese cousins are even older. I guess that playfulness is a cure to ageing! Regarding my evolution, I am still used very often in

Q & A WITH

graphic workshops and other such places. I am
less popular than before, but when you have had
such a long life it is understandable to have long
ups and downs. I would say that I am more of an
odd case now. People use me for my artistic properties rather than as a printing technique to reproduce images. The tactility I carry is very specific
and does not suit all kinds of images, and even less
book illustrations you know.

JP Indeed, I remember that... isn't it because of the
wood structure? I mean, could you explain how you
work and how the sensation of the wood is a big
part in your process?

X Well, my « process » as you could call it, is quite
close to any other kind of engraving technique, yet
much rougher and less sensitive. My masters have
to carve their images onto my skin with a gouge.
There are all sorts of gouges which are sharp
knifes with different curves that allow the creation
of a big range of patterns and textures. They are
very manual, and have funny looking shapes.
Unlike woodblock prints, the carving is done along
the grain of my skin. After the image is created,
I can finally be covered with ink. You can't imagine
how nice it feels. And then I am pressed onto the
paper, the ink penetrating both of us. Yes, tthis is
how the image is created. The bottom line is, I am

MR. XYLOGRAPHY

a very hands-on process, with a lot of similarities to other engraving techniques, yet my materiality gives me a very independent identity!

JP But is having a strong identity not all right? How do you see yourself facing the post digital era? How can you actually compete with fast, efficient and precise workers such as inkjet?

X Well, as you said, they are very serious, modern and effective, which are aspects that are only positive in the spectrum of cost-effectiveness and profit making. Who said I wanted to go there? Let's be honest, people will always need to do stuff for the sake of pure self-expression and pleasure. And then I will be there! And if I have to disappear because people are too busy being productive, then I would not want to live anymore anyway!

JP Such a dark way to end this interview Xylo, I hope I did not force dark thoughts into your brain... And don't worry, I think there will always be creative and passionate people to use you!

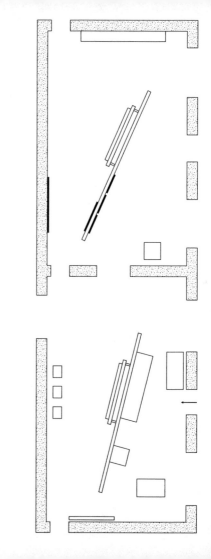

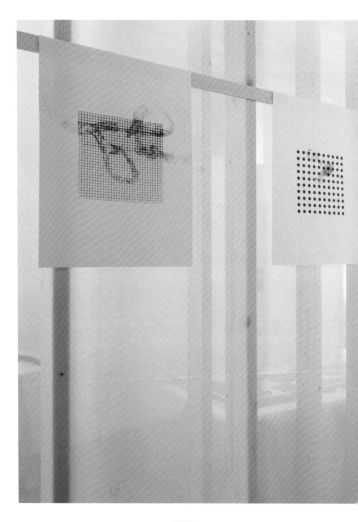

P. 169, 171

Lieven De Boeck
Sense and Nonsense, 2015
Created at Frans Masereel
Centrum, Collection of the artist.
Lasercut on goatskin,
silkscreen on plastic,
Ca. 75 x 115 cm, ca. 42 x 60 cm

Language and materiality seem
to diffuse in the silent sacrality
of Lieven De Boeck's work. In
this piece the skin (of a goat)
can be seen as a symbol for
human tactility and moves us
away from the culture present
around our bodies – and made
visible in the plastic garbage
bag 'Nonsense'.

P. 172-173

Semâ Berikovic
Untitled (trails), 2015
Created at Frans Masereel
Centrum, Courtesy by Gallery
Stigter van Doesburg.
Silkscreen, snailtrails 40 x 50 cm

Sema Bekirovic made several
silk screens and collaborated
with a bunch of snails. Snails
are extremely tactile: where we
mostly touch the worldaround
us only with the very ends of our
bodies, the snail does so with
a maximum of body surface.

When the snails crawl across
the freshly made prints, their
slime trails dissolve the (water
soluble) paint, leaving coloured
trails on the paper.

P. 175

Matthieu Blanchard
Esthesia (trails), 2015
Collection of the artist, Created
at Frans Masereel Centrum.
Laser cut on painting on canvas,
15,5 x 12,5 cm

In these pieces Matthieu Blanchard worked on the pathology
affecting tactility. He somehow
considers painting as a disease,
in the sense that it contaminates
a surface. 'Hypoesthesia' and
'hyperesthesia' respectively
mean weakened sensitivity/tacti-
lity and an increased sensitivity/
tactility. The two pieces that
were produced are the result of
the aggression of the material
as a surface.

P. 176-177

Frederic Geurts
Study, 2015
Collection of the artist,
Created at Frans Masereel
Centrum. Soft ground etching
technique on Zerkall lythopaper,
76 x 56 cm

The three etchings were made by means of the soft ground etching technique in which a thin sheet of paper is put onto a copper plate that is covered with a layer of soft varnish. As with carbon paper the lines drawn onto the paper remove the varnish from the plate. On these very lines the acid can reach the plate and corrode it. As a result, the act of drawing is very direct and due to the structure of the paper the lines resemble pencil marks. The motifs/drawings are spatial studies.

P. 178-179

Ulrike Mohr
Meteoritenpapier, 2015
Carbon Paper, 2015
Created at Frans Masereel Centrum. Installation of various carbonized meteor papers, Lasercut on carbon paper, Various dimensions

If wood can be carbonized, then so can the fibres of paper. Carbon paper, then again, is a different form of captured carbon. Both materials of graphic culture are carriers of cultivation by man. The heat of the carbonization process models paper into an extremely light object, that looks somewhat like a topographical map. While working with carbonized paper, the artist was thinking about stories by Charles Fort, an American writer and researcher of anomalous phenomena, describing a rain of carbon papers falling from the sky. This is where the title 'Meteoritenpapier' comes from.

P. 181

Thomas Rentmeister
Untitled, 2015
Created at Frans Masereel Centrum, Collection of Thomas Rentmeister, Courtesy by Ellen de Bruijne Projects, Amsterdam.
Etching, ink on paper
107,5 x 75,5 cm

After making some soft ground etchings with underwear pieces, Thomas Rentmeister decided to use now digital technology to extend his etching practice. He high-end scanned a piece of underwear. The large scale print of the textile structure was transferred through a chemical process onto a big copper plate. In the acid bath a relief of the texture emerged. The print itself has a certain blurring and blotchiness, caused by the higher quantity of production steps, the digital editing and the enlargement.

Dear,

Reading and touching this book, you've engaged with thoughts and artistic works related to the tactile phenomenon, through the specific practice of print making. I've felt privileged to connect with these in the developing process, a dynamic of progressive doubt in the development, of engagement to the matter and the expression in the result, which is reflected in the book itself.

What triggered me to engage the conceptual wonder about the notion of tactility was that many people said the books and exhibitions I'm involved in making are so 'wonderfully tactile'. Hearing this made me realise I was apparently producing something inarticulate, something that was playing people's hearts and minds – and somehow I felt uncomfortable with this compliment… Therefore my main concern was critical and regarded the 'wonderfulness' of tactility. Because it is rather ephemeral, possibly even a myth, I'm suspect to wonder who would stand to benefit from this myth. But in order to answer this, we need to know if there is a reality to tactility beyond the habitually paired adjective of the 'wonderful'.

Something we had to face, aside from the measure of control over our fascinations, was the issue of digitalisation. Evidently, as the brain is hot-wired into a world of digital tactility, our physical sense is being sidestepped. As Alessandro Ludevico, editor of Neural magazine and know for his thinking on the post-digital and print, describes, the capacity to surpass the material world by an immaterial one is yet to come. Meanwhile we can and do enjoy the actual qualities of, for instance, printed matter. The question whether we will transfer our emotional investment from matter to immateriality is yet to be decided. This presents a continuously developing range of qualities, as Esther Krop of De Monsterkamer, showroom for print, describes in regard to newly available types of paper and more.

Art writer Lars Bang Larsen describes how a graphic reproduction always results in unique copies as a singularity of glitches, and is therefore less of an opposite to a unique art work than a digital reproduction. And, like an artwork, it is the result of a direct agency of the artist. The work, as processed material, will always 'bear witness to the will of the material vis-à-vis intentionality'. In a way, he argues, making print such as woodcuts is "the most uncool thing" as it – in my words – steps out of a dialectical chain of progress and actuality (in time). To return to Bang Larsen: "In the print, effects are slow and affect becomes tactile and palpable. Sceptical." So here, according to him, the material and its processing become an act to reframe art historical and contemporary time within printed matter, possibly even the time-based notions in popular culture, as context through which we perceive and position the material imagery.

Where Bang Larsen articulates the dynamic positioning of processed material in changing times, UCLA connected art thinker and independent art maker

Johanna Drucker touches upon how material also co-authors and - to speculate beyond this point. This also leads to a reduction in control within production by the author/artist, as well as with regard to ascribed authorship after delivery of the work - something many artists will acknowledge - and possibly even places the visual result in the eye of the beholder to become some sort of anthropocentric solitude (something I hope to explore in a follow up of this project).

It is here that the artistic processing in the course of the residency, by selected artists whose work has a specific materiality at its core, becomes relevant: specialists in the poetic range of their material vocabulary, I wanted to highlight.

After ruining one goatskin with a laser, Lieven De Boeck had to find another one to make a second attempt. The objective of burning a modest imprint of the word 'sense', written backwards, into the skin by laser turned out pretty much according to the programme's algorithm. However, the hue and the spacing and perspective on the skin were yet to be considered, since the skin is different form a straight-angle canvass with a top and a bottom. The texture of the paper was very much relevant to Thomas Rentmeister, who struggled with a print of the cropped magnification of linen underwear – the classic underwear- to the fibres of the paper, indeed slowing "things" down, in line with Bang Larsen's thoughts. Ulrike Mohr is firing wooden objects in a sealed-off pit to carbonise them, they shrink and become a deep black. Because she releases a rigid destruction without controlling the firing process the result is nothing less than the outcome. The objects themselves, however, originate from specific grounds and release a strong physical relationship. Semâ Berikovic also releases nature, but as a chance process in the form of snails that become uncontrollable painters on a grid of ink that they disturb with randomly curving and crossing lines (random, unless you put faith in the snail-author).

It makes this piece a rather conceptual one, allowing the voice of nature to enter. As an alchemist, creator/author and visual deliverer, Matthieu Blanchard brought chemicals and more to be alloyed on canvas, making him the vehicle of a holistic magic, rather than the man-author or nature-transmitter. Finally, Frederic Geurts played the cards of perspective and minimalism to set out for a time-based structural ambiguity, a kind of abstract tactility to the eye of the beholder, triggered by an optical mind fuck with the material structures he proposes.

The graphic processing by these artists differed in the manner they position their relationship as authors to the material they used or, vice versa, turned themselves into vehicles for the material itself. In case of materially motivated stances (those rather mystical) a practice's vocabulary has its own material semantics. In case of a practice-motivated stance (those rather anthropocentric conceptual ones) every practice's semantics has its own vocabulary. As art critic

Camiel van Winkel described in 'The Regime of Visibility', these are two sides of one and the same coin. As conversations and production proceeded, it often appeared difficult to consider things beyond the 'wonderful'. The romantic sensibility to dwell in tingles and shivers brought on by encounters of a fundamentally existential nature were strong. It adhered to what philosopher Rik Peters describes as the 'body that sees through its eyes', or to the fact that by positive interactions, through actively touching and reaching out, we invest in our relationship with the world, as Dr Marieke Sonneveld of TU Delft argues.

While the production took place at the graphic workplace Frans Masereel Centre, it reached out with an exhibition at Z33. First of all, to eyes perceiving all the works and all the deceiving visual qualities of tactility that came along. Secondly, to the art-historical and contemporary-artistic information brought in by visitors the work itself and additional texts: the contagious expert ideas. In this way the experience of the tactile spectrum offered many connections to include on site.

The project releases a blending of matter: of the perceiving body (viewer), the producing body (artists and authors) and the produced body (the artwork). What became evident in the above is the instrumentalisation of anthropocentricity to our eye and to our mind through the release of matter, and the opportunity of visual/sculptural dissent, rather then finding peaceful comfort. On top of this, emancipated citizenship seems to be an illusion in the everlasting changes of times, along with technological and cultural connections that produce yet more complexity. This is anticipated by independent minds and practices as well as by the driving force – call it the technocratic apparatus of post-capitalism. It can be a source for us to find awareness and more riches.

Clearly, the issue of tactility is the tissue of both control and self-governance. As it contributes to the argument put forth by Ta-Nehisi Coates, of the black body's exploitation by the white coloured apparatus, I am inclined to connect this bio-political current (bio-political, as an increasing material entrapment of our body that disciplines the mind while it plays with our body's senses) to a wider problem of citizenship within technocratic post-capitalism. We cannot reject it but should live our lives and relate, by exploring our sensory experience in order to make sense of the world and engaging the material poetics of our environment. It is for this reason that I happily include the elaborate essay on materiality and bio-politics in the era of globalisation by Christopher Breu, associate professor at the Illinois State University.

I'm happy to end on a positive note and a little push to empowerment. As Drucker says: 'Leaving a trace, even if it vanishes eventually, provides the illusion that you can hold onto something in the flux and change of life.' So: even though our sense for poetics might be taken hostage by something larger than life, something beyond our daily encounters, and though anthropocentricity oriented towards abstraction is defining material orders according to rationality – or not – and trying to open up our lives to the spiritual forces in the holistic bodily spheres, we can levitate at will and try, and engage with our hearts and have our minds follow up on those encounters. It might be for this reason that tactility, as a possibly radically conservative totem to literally hold on to, can offer critical refuge and open up to a new grounding in our direct sphere of living.

The quest led to a distant position, let it be the opposite side of the same coin. Simply: by activating sensibilities we can relate better. In the end we may live our lives to the max.

*Can you feel it? *

Freek Lomme, initiator
and host of the project.

COLOPHON

Set Margins' #1

ISBN 978-90-832706-0-9

Editor and curator
    Freek Lomme

Editorial and
curatorial advisors
    Evelien Bracke - Z33
    Jan Boelen - Z33
    Sofie Dederen - FMC

Graphic design
    Bureau Vielcazat

Authors
    Lars Bang Larsen
    Christopher Breu
    Johanna Drucker
    Alessandro Ludovico
    Esther Krop
    Juliette Pepin
    Rik Peters
    Marieke Sonneveld

Artists
    Sema Bekirovic
    Matthieu Blanchard
    Lieven De Boeck
    Frederic Geurts
    Thomas Rentmeister
    Ulrike Mohr

Translations
    Laurence Schertz
    Nanne op 't Ende

Photography exhibition Z33
    Kristof Vranken

Project assistant
    Juliette Pépin

Special thanks to
    Sofie Dederen - FMC
    Isabelle Vanhoutte - FMC
    Ivan Durt - FMC
    Evelien Bracke - Z33
    Jan Boelen - Z33
    Harvey Herman
    All involved artists
    and authors

Printing
    Raddraaier

Fonts
    ITC Century Std
    Akzidenz Grotesk Pro

Third print
    1000 copies, Sep. 2022

This print is fully made
possible by Private investment
of Freek Lomme and
the support of Pierre Martin

Publisher
    Set Margins'
    www.setmargins.press